The
Road to
Equity

The
Road to
Equity

GENDER, ETHNICITY, AND LANGUAGE

Impolitic Essays

Brian Lee Crowley

Foreword by Eric Kierans

First published in 1994 by
Stoddart Publishing Co. Limited
34 Lesmill Road
Toronto, Canada
M3B 2T6
(416) 445-3333

Canadian Cataloguing in Publication Data

Crowley, Brian Lee
The road to equity: gender, ethnicity, and language

ISBN 0-7737-5640-X

1. Canada — Social conditions — 1971 — I. Title.

FC89.C76 1994   971.064'7   C94-930033-0
F1021.2.C76 1994

Cover concept: Angel Guerra
Cover design: Brant Cowie/ArtPlus Limited
Typesetting: Tony Gordon Ltd.

Printed and bound in Canada

*Stoddart Publishing gratefully acknowledges the support
of the Canada Council, Ontario Ministry of Culture,
Tourism, and Recreation, Ontario Arts Council, and
Ontario Publishing Centre in the development of writing
and publishing in Canada.*

Contents

Foreword

THE SINGLE MOST IMPORTANT QUESTION that has ever been asked is, in my view, "Am I my brother's keeper?" It is not a religious question only; it covers all aspects of living and meaning, all spheres of activity, the political and the economic, the social and the cultural and, of course, the spiritual and the moral.

Cain, of course, had answered this question before he hurled it at the Lord, for he had already murdered his brother. No, he was not his brother's keeper. He had no responsibility for his brother. He was for himself and no one else.

The question divides society and the future in two. There can be no quibbling with the answer. One either is or is not his brother's keeper. A "No" answer means chaos and destruction of the right to live in a social context. This is what happened to Cain. Said the Lord, "a fugitive and a wanderer shall you be on the earth." A "No" is the denial of community and responsibility; it is every man for himself — competition, conflict, and confusion. It threatens extremes such as we have today: widespread poverty, pollution of nature, and degrading unemployment, side-by-side with unlimited wealth, power, and domination. In *Democracy in America*, Alexis de Tocqueville described this egoism as the ultimate reality of a society that would throw man "back forever upon himself alone."

A "Yes" answer is consistent not only with Judeo–Christian tradition, but with all religious thought and tradition. Writes Fazlur Rahman, Professor of Islamic Thought, University of Chicago: "There is no such thing as a societiless individual." Man and his activities are meaningful only in a community context.

The truest and most complete sense of community has been well expressed by Moses ben Maimon (Maimonides), who outlined eight degrees of charity, laws of moral behaviour, and justice. The eighth stated that "The highest type of charity is the prevention of poverty by providing a poor man with a means of livelihood." In my view, there could be no truer interpretation of the meaning of "brother's keeper" than this law.

My own sense of what is going on in modern society is this. The social, political, and economic drives at work ignore the ultimate values that alone can make national and international communities work. Collectively, we behave as Cain, the first child ever born, behaved. We are greedy. Whatever the scene, we want it all, to be number one, to be the master of all things, of nature, and of people. To be number one means to take the means necessary to achieve that goal. Reason takes over and the calculation of higher and lower prices rationalizes and instrumentalizes all living and non-living things.

In such a world, the measure of all things is money. The world is composed of those who have money and those who have little or none. As Hegel pointed out, people with money are real, people without it are not: "A person is real to the extent to which he has money. . . . The formal principle of reason is to be found here . . . It is the abstraction from all particularity, character, historicity, etc. of the individual."

But what good is economics, what good is the political state, if it cannot solve the basic problem of living: making employment and a useful life possible for all people?

The social cost of unemployment in modern society has led to a whole host of derivative calamities that affect affluent and poor communities alike, ranging from insecurity and alienation, to welfare and dependency, to government incompetence and political corruption. On the personal level there have emerged such evils as crime, the drug culture, and the cluster of problems grouped under Brian Lee Crowley's sex, lies, and violence. On the level of the nation state we witness the decline of morality and the social order, the crumbling of democratic values and institutions such as the market, and "the obsolescence of politics as a civilized pursuit." There also has been a continuous decline in trust and confidence in political leadership and government since the early 1970s. There are two main reasons for this. People believe that political figures are motivated more by their own enrichment in terms of power and money than in improving the condition of their communities. Secondly, with the decline of the political state, its place has been taken by the corporate and technological power blocs. In other words, there is little that governments can do in the face of the accumulated financial and corporate power that is leading nations into the new technological world of entertainment, gimmicks, and gadgets.

Unhappily, the Canadian government is itself a supreme example of the powerlessness of the political state. It has repeatedly proven itself unable to cope with more than eleven percent unemployment and a net public debt exceeding half a trillion dollars. In his recent budget speech, the minister of finance, Paul Martin, noted that our net public debt reached $511 billion this year, a ratio of debt to a Gross Domestic Product of $711 billion of seventy-two percent, a condition that leaves the government no room to maneuver and at the mercy of financial and corporate power, both domestic and international. In 1974, the unemployment rate was 5.3 percent and the net public debt was $25 billion for a ratio of nineteen percent to the GDP for that year. In the period of *two decades*, Canadians, through their government, have increased their net public debt by nearly half a trillion dollars. The question then arises in all its ugliness: Does any generation have the moral right to live on a scale so far beyond its means, knowing full well that future generations, our children, will be burdened with the back-breaking costs of paying for our extravagance?

Governments are elected to provide their people with a rational organization of their lives and a reasonable standard of living across the entire community. No society can long survive that cannot find useful work for its people and that mortgages its future with crushing debt. When this happens, a nation becomes fragmented and tribalized, and particularities of gender, ethnicity, and language explode, as Brian Lee Crowley points out in his reflections on the erosion and decay in Canadian democracy.

Crowley's book is a critical and unsparing analysis of major distortions in Canadian social and political institutions, caused by the incompetence and incomprehension of our political leaders. Indeed, the five essays are a stinging indictment of the failure of governments and institutions to keep pace with and face up to rapid cultural change. In *Pour une Réforme de l'Entreprise* (1963), François Bloch-Lainé wrote about this very problem: *"Dans la plupart des domains, les faits one été plus vites que les idées et les institutions sont en rétard sur les pratiqués."*

Crowley does not refrain from criticizing those who justify change with one-line ethical slogans or utilitarian judgements that determine what is right according to what yields the greatest good for the greatest number. Crowley is a tough thinker as befits one who sees himself as both a utilitarian and a skeptic.

Crowley's "Racism, Property, and Aboriginal Culture" reveals how the government's dealings with the First Nations have been a mess. It has been give, give, give. Yet the government doesn't demand anything in return as the aboriginal groups tell us whether they want to be part of a liberal democratic society or to revert to their ten-thousand-year-old culture. Ovide Mercredi, it seems, wants both.

In Crowley's essay on free markets versus central planning, "The Vindication of Doubt," he concludes that there are problems "that neither governments nor markets can really influence satisfactorily. Markets may be better than we thought, and governments rather worse. The reality is that the case for caution and skepticism about all institutions is stronger . . ." Nowhere is this more true than in the continuing decline of trust and credibility in government, politics, and political leadership. Politics has become virtually powerless to effect real change, its place assumed by commercial and financial power. Six years hence we are promised superhighways, technological products, and information systems if government support and private investment can be harnessed to the challenge. To produce what? Gadgets and gimmicks, while the real needs are food, housing, and clothing. Such innovations promise productivity, competitiveness, and the redundancy of workers when the real challenge we must face is unemployment. If we follow the superhighway we could end up on the road to nowhere.

Let us give E.F. Schumacher the last word: "What is the meaning of democracy, freedom, human dignity, standard of living, self-realization, fulfilment? Is it a matter of goods or of people? Of course, it is a matter of people." Brian Lee Crowley would agree, as he also deals with the institutions that have failed people, which is one of the many reasons you should read these five sparkling essays.

ERIC KIERANS

Preface

IN 1991–92 CANADA went through the most recent of its constitutional paroxysms in the form of the so-called Canada Round negotiations, which resulted in the Charlottetown Accord. As the Secretary to the Kierans Committee, Nova Scotia's Working Group on the Constitution, and then as that province's constitutional adviser during the Canada Round, I was intimately involved in the whole process, just as I had been five years earlier as constitutional adviser to the Manitoba government during the Meech Lake round.

History records that the ill starred Charlottetown agreement was defeated in the October 1992 referendum. Wearied by the intensity of the negotiations and deeply troubled by much that I had seen and heard during those talks, as well as during the referendum campaign, I took a year's leave of absence from teaching in the Political Science Department of Dalhousie University. My original thought was to take that time to reflect and write on what I had learned about the Constitution and how we think about that document in this country.

It soon became apparent to me, however, that what was troubling me went much further than the way we talk about our constitutional arrangements. In our political life generally it seemed that governments were constantly being solicited to think of Canadians in one-dimensional terms. The complexity of our individual lives was being reduced to simplistic generalizations; to governments more and more we were becoming anglophones, francophones, Québécois, aboriginals, women, or visible minorities, and less and less unique individuals. Tribalism and collectivism were being exalted.

The ebb and flow of politics often moves between the poles of individualism and collectivism, but I had the impression that the very ideas of individual liberty, in the sense of classical political and economic liberalism, were falling into disuse in Canada's political life. Canadians are very individualistic, but to say so is to commit a kind of social solecism; to celebrate that individualism and draw from it guiding principles about how we ought to be governed is to make oneself unfit for polite company.

Yet I could not shake the conviction that individualism, both political and economic, is the only foundation on which true civility can be built, and I decided to try and show why I believe this to be the case in this series of essays. Each one takes some central issue of Canadian politics — the Constitution, aboriginal self-government, sex and violence, and pay and employment equity — and makes an explicit argument for a liberal-individualist way of understanding and dealing with that issue in opposition to the collectivist impulse. The final essay about the life and work of F.A. Hayek is included to help the reader situate my approach in a larger political, economic, and philosophical context.

Many people have read and commented on some or all of the essays. I would like in particular to thank John Kavanagh, John Richards, Alastair Saunders, Ron Watts, Bob Finbow, Henry Milner, Randy Litchfield, Bill Gairdner, and Don Bastian for their comments and encouragement. As well as commenting on the other essays, Ian Porter was instrumental in the completion of the Hayek piece. My friend Eric Kierans, whom I have come to know well because of our work together on the Constitution, was good enough to write the foreword, for which I am most grateful. Parts of the essay on employment equity appeared in the November 1993 issue of *Canadian Business*. It goes without saying that I bear sole responsibility for the ideas expressed in *The Road to Equity*.

Of course, my greatest recognition and gratitude go to Alan Beattie, who gives me courage, and Berthe Dirren, who gives me strength. This book is dedicated to them both, a very small payment on some very large debts.

Sex, Lies, and Violence

The web of our life is of a mingled yarn, good and ill together.
Our virtues would be proud if our faults whipt them not;
and our crimes would despair if they were not cherish'd
  by our virtues.

All's Well That Ends Well

WINTER IN MONTREAL has its pleasures, but they were far from everyone's mind on December 6, 1989. The icy fingers of the season were gripping the city hard that day, and under the sombre sky a heavy snow was falling. It was the kind of cutting, bone-numbing chill that makes one stay indoors, if possible, and feel vaguely heroic when confronting the cold, trudging heavily through the wind to a destination always too far away.

Night falls in late afternoon in early December. It was out of this almost preternatural gloom that a man named Marc Lépine strode purposefully into l'École Polytechnique, the engineering school of the Université de Montréal. He was carrying a rifle. He had come to kill women.

By the time he had finished his rampage in the corridors and classrooms of the Polytechnique, fourteen women students lay dead, several others were wounded, and Lépine had shot himself to death. Montreal and the country as a whole were plunged into almost stupefied anguish and self-examination. The significance of what had happened seemed all too apparent: the rage and violence that men feel towards women had overwhelmed Lépine, and he had acted out what lurks in the dark side of every male psyche.

The National Film Board documentary *After the Montreal Massacre* gave eloquent voice to this theme. It showed a queue of hundreds of people waiting to pay their respects to the murdered women. A mother expressed the fear women feel and the danger posed by men: "I feel as if it happened to myself, as if I or my daughter were in that room . . . He was a maniac, but it's just a magnification of what's happening to women all the time." The sentiment was echoed by Sylvie Gagnon, one of the survivors of the shooting: "Lépine is a symbol of death and hate . . . he is a problem, not an individual."

Of Vice and Men

IF EVER A SINGLE EVENT could be said to have awakened a society from its dogmatic slumbers, this was it. Suddenly, the problem of violence against women, in all its forms, was given a focus and a face. Rape, wife-battering, violence against women, all the forms of male abuse of women suddenly were made monstrously concrete and undeniable for everyone, men and women alike. A seachange in public attitudes occurred, and a new moral equilibrium was struck between the sexes, in which men could no longer avoid responsibility for their systematic campaign of violence against women.

Voices that had long been raised in righteous indignation and outrage against this violence were now part of the mainstream of public debate, and the international campaign against violence against women suddenly took on a new urgency in Canada. An unnamed female professor at an Alberta university is reported to have said in a public lecture that men have been masquerading as human beings. Canadian feminist scholar Susan Cole suggested that "men have to look at the rapist inside of them." Well-known

American feminist Andrea Dworkin, exhorted women to "get [abusive men] killed," and the film *After the Montreal Massacre* featured lecturer and writer Charlotte Bunch saying that the war on women is a "civil emergency."

The indictment against men goes well beyond the horrific actions of Marc Lépine and is captured in a plethora of statistics. The figures are too well-known to need repetition, so one will do: one million women in Canada are battered each year by their (male) partners. The sordid truth is finally coming out of the closet and into the open. Men and their attitudes are the source of a systematic campaign of terror and violence against women. The problem has become known simply as "male violence," and it seems that only a top-to-bottom transformation of society will set it to rights, including a rewriting of history, control of the content of books, films, and other media, root and branch reform of our economy and political institutions, and especially a remoulding of the male mind.

Before such moral certainty and a clear program based on seemingly unassailable facts, it may seem churlish to call for a moment's reflection. It may even be male denial of a crippling burden of guilt. On the other hand, a moral panic that will not brook quiet examination on the grounds of guilt alone is suspect. And there are other grounds for suspicion of the campaign against male violence against women: suspicion about the facts that are presented to us, about their interpretation, and about the understanding of violence — its sources and its significance — that underlies this campaign.

All victims of unmerited and unsolicited violence deserve our moral sympathy and support. But on that score statistics tell us unambiguously that many more individual men than individual women are actually in need of our sympathy and protection. To focus on "violence against women" is to transfer an appropriate sympathy for individual female victims of violence to an entire group that in itself comprises victims, non-victims, and perpetrators.

This generalization is just as much a caricature of the truth as its opposite, that a group composed of the good, the bad, and the indifferent, such as men, is uniquely responsible and worthy of moral blame for violence.

To have any hope of success in tackling a problem like violence, the first order of business is to have a clear view of what the problem is. We must begin by considering exactly why violence *is* a proper object of social concern.

A Brief History of Violence

THERE WAS A TIME WHEN VIOLENCE between people, while morally blameworthy, was simply a fact of life. The greater offences were punished, especially when the victims were the rich and powerful, who had a high opinion of themselves and, therefore, of the sanctity of their person. Drunken brawls were more likely to prompt charges of disturbing the peace and damage to property than of assault. We often forget that the efficacious modern state, whose agents apply the law with reasonable effectiveness, is precisely that: modern. Thomas Hobbes's *Leviathan* recalls a not-so-distant time when life was "solitary, poore, nasty, brutish and short" *because* individuals were free to use violence in the pursuit of their desires. In the absence of effective civil and criminal remedies, injuries to person, reputation, or property were properly and summarily dealt with by private violence and vendetta. Montagues and Capulets offered a rough-and-ready alternative to the sometimes impotent Prince of Verona.

The state's monopoly on the legitimate use of force was, as Hobbes argued, the necessary condition of any progress for humanity, because it guaranteed that the fruits of our labours could not arbitrarily be taken from us (except, of course, by the state itself, but that is another problem). We were free to plan for the long term. The preservation of that freedom was, however, a purely practical reason for controlling violence. A social and intellectual revolution was needed before the *moral* condemnation of violence could really have much bite. That revolution, which reached its fullest flowering in the Enlightenment, gave rise to that great hallmark of Western civilization: the belief that individuals are free and equal because they are endowed with a moral personality.

Violence against individuals became the object of righteous indignation and condemnation because it was the most obvious, direct, and crude denial of individual conscience. Violence treated individuals as mere objects, tools that one coerced to do one's will without consent. If all moral value springs from the capacity of each of us to make free and informed choices for ourselves about our lives, what more heinous moral crime could there be than the violence that destroys such freedom? The ethical strength of our denunciation of violence is, therefore, inseparable from our ethical commitment to the equal worth of individuals, whatever the superficial differences that distinguish them.

We all know intuitively that the problem to be confronted with respect to violence is the denial of individual freedom and dignity. When it becomes necessary to use violence, as in wartime, most of us have a deep psychological need to depersonalize the enemy forces, to deny them the complex features of their individuality, to make them guilty and inhuman Gooks or Commies, Krauts or Nazis. The need for this is well accepted, and was the principal reason for the severe criticism of the officers in charge during the famous World War I impromptu Christmas Day party between Allied and German troops. It is infinitely harder to kill a man into whose face you've looked, a man with whom you've toasted the Christmas spirit, and whose children you've seen in a photograph. It makes him too real as an individual. But far from signaling a moral failing, both the need for such depersonalization and the inevitable criticism of it are signs of a society whose ethics are in good order. Normally we cannot think of killing other individuals, because it is degrading, disgraceful, and dehumanizing. But when

survival or some other paramount social good is physically men-
aced, it sometimes becomes a deeply regrettable necessity. A way
around the usual moral standards is needed, but the fact of such a
departure makes it liable to criticism, and when the shortlived
overriding imperative of war ceases, so, too, must acts of aggression towards the former enemy.

Contrast this understanding of wartime violence with the practice of the great dogmatic "isms," or ideologies, of our time:
fascism, Nazism, communism, racism, and radical feminism,* to
name just a few. Their whole reason for existence, their whole
"analysis," is based on a "true understanding" of the workings of
impersonal forces whose operation permanently disfigures society
and denies freedom to its members. Beside these forces, individual
identity and choice are illusory, mere phantoms of the brain. A
picture is painted of society as the site of a constantly renewed
battle between two irreconcilably opposed interests; much more
than just the moral equivalent of war, it is the real thing, but carried
on by institutional means.

One group (for example, capitalists, Jews, men) is seen to guard
and represent a "system" whose sole justification is the group's
enrichment and aggrandizement at the expense of the rest. All the
usual characteristics necessary to their dehumanization are attributed to this group: facelessness, corruption, moral enormities, cruel
exploitation of the weak. To the equally anonymous rest (proletar-
ians, Aryans, women) are attributed overriding virtue and heroism
as befits those who by definition are not only wholly innocent of
wrongdoing, but also alone can rid the world of evil.

According to Isaiah Berlin, as early as 1848 Alexander Herzen,

---

* I hesitated a long time before adding the adjective "radical" to "feminism," especially
when all the other ideologies are presented in their unadorned states. The decision to
do so was based primarily on the fact that the feminist movement is a complex and
ideologically diverse one; it would seem wrong to imply that the attitudes I am decrying
are shared by all those who describe themselves as feminists. In all later references in
this essay to feminism, the adjective "radical" is implied.

the Russian radical, had understood the bitter harvest that would spring from the seed of such a caricature of the complexity of human society and human motivation. That harvest was human sacrifice with a good conscience. He said that a new form of human sacrifice had arisen in his time, one of living human beings on the altars of abstractions — nation, church, party, class, progress, the forces of history — which have all been invoked in his day and in ours. Dogmatic belief in such abstractions depersonalizes *everyone* by making them mere puppets of social forces they neither control nor influence directly. It makes violence, therefore, easier for all to utilize. Both perpetrators and victims become less than human because they are not permitted to have the full dimensions of real people. They have no private thoughts, no intentions, no responsibility for their actions. The "real" author of violence is an abstract system, which merely acts through people. The victims, too, are members of a mass — individuals whose violation is best understood through "systemic factors," through what they have in common, rather than through what makes them individuals. Finally, those who use violence against the system, against the oppressors, are merely the instruments of liberation, the foot soldiers of history, whose only responsibility is to a far-off but ideal future. The moral focus on violence is first blurred and then shifted, with predictable consequences for our traditional view of responsibility, individual action, blame, and punishment.

We all want moral certainty and simplicity; we all want to be on the side that is entirely right and against those who are entirely wrong. To do that we must simplify. But let's be clear about what is being simplified away in these ideologies: the crucial bridge between any system and each human action. That bridge is an individual human mind, personality, and will. That bridge has intentions, desires, and beliefs, and cannot be relieved of individual responsibility. To deny individual responsibility is to encourage, and indeed to invite, violence by teaching us that responsibility is an illusion and, therefore, that any moral enormity is allowed.

Lépine's Legacy

A FRIEND AND COLLEAGUE, on considering this description, objected to seeing radical feminism included in the list of caricaturing ideologies. After all, fourteen women *were* killed by a gunman at the École Polytechnique in Montreal, and that is compelling supporting evidence of the feminist analysis of men's violence against women by men and of the existence of an exploitative "patriarchal" system. Because we all want to identify ourselves with the outpouring of grief, rage, and revulsion that followed this horrific act, it is tempting to agree. But, in fact, what Marc Lépine did confirms precisely the case being made here, and shows the danger of an uncritical acceptance of the now conventional interpretation of that event.

After all, Marc Lépine himself clearly believed in the dehumanizing dogmatic group analysis. He accepted that society is a battleground in which men and women marshal their forces against one another in a competition for power that one group can only win at the expense of the other. As a man, Lépine was entitled to status, power, and money; he didn't have to earn them as an individual. If he didn't have them it had to be due to their being taken from him by the competition: women. Since women were to him anonymous, faceless, and interchangeable members of the opposition, vengeance taken on any of them for his male-group humiliation was vengeance taken on all.

Not only did Lépine assume that he could know the enemy by their reproductive equipment, but also that he could know their thoughts without knowing them as persons. How else are we to understand the fact that he did more than merely single out women at the Polytechnique? He knew that these women had to be feminists; they had to have certain beliefs. Never mind that Nathalie Provost, who survived the shooting, cried out to him in vain that they were *not* feminists. This was too complicated a message, for it invited him to learn about the complexity of their lives, about the many hopes, dreams, and aspirations that had led each of those young human beings to be at the Polytechnique. His action depended crucially on not having to confront a critical truth: that they were not there because they happened to be women; they were there because they wanted to be engineers and had what it took to succeed. Indeed, like Provost, many are angered by the appropriation of this event by ideologues who also want to wipe out the individual identities that made those young women who they were, remembering them instead for Lépine's reason: that they were all female.

The other side of this, of course, is the strikingly similar assumptions made by certain feminists (of both sexes) about the event and its actors. Rallying to the same cry, "by their genitals ye shall know them," the ideologues divine that the fact that Marc Lépine possessed a penis tells us everything we need to know in order to understand his action and attribute responsibility for it. His beliefs, no matter how monstrous, no matter how vigorously opposed and rejected by the vast bulk of people of both sexes, can safely be assumed to be shared by men, either consciously or unconsciously. As another of his victims who survived, Sylvie Gagnon, put it, "Lépine is a symbol of death and hate . . . he is a problem, not an individual."

To see the Polytechnique massacre in this way, as a feminist or women's issue, to see it as an attack by a member of "the other" group and, therefore, as further evidence supporting a belief in patriarchy, as further evidence of the irreconcilable interests opposing men and women, is to say, not to put too fine a point on it, that Lépine was right. To place the emphasis on the *women* students makes it a *women's* tragedy, in exactly the same way that one can see deaths of Catholics in the Shankill Road district of Belfast as a Catholic tragedy, deaths of blacks in Soweto as a black tragedy, and deaths of Muslims in Bosnia as a Muslim tragedy, rather than the human tragedies that they all are. They are human tragedies because in each case it is the dehumanization of individuals through their easy assimilation into some convenient anonymous group that makes the killings possible.

By the same token, to assume that all men have a Marc Lépine inside them because they are men is to deny the importance of the individual mind, which is the necessary link between system and action. Some Ulster Protestants kill Catholics. Most don't. Some white South Africans kill blacks. Most don't. We cannot begin to understand the difference without taking the time, trouble, and patience to unravel each life as it is linked to those around it. To make the accidents of life by which we can arbitrarily be classified (factors like sex, language, race, nationality, or religion) more important than the common humanity that binds us together is to say to Lépine that he was right, that what women have is at the expense of men. The alternative is to say that we all gain when human beings are able to develop their talents and abilities by their own efforts, without being prevented from doing so by morally unjustifiable obstacles based on purely contingent factors such as the ones I've just enumerated.

The surest token of the moral seriousness of a rejection and disapproval of violence is, then, a focus on the individual who is its victim. What is blameworthy in violence is its denial of an individual's liberty and dignity, of the free choices each of us makes in building a life that is truly our own. One can leave that sure ground by almost imperceptible but glaringly arbitrary steps. In the case of violence and women, one such step is to focus attention exclusively on violence performed against women, making violence done to *them* the wrong, or at least the most important one. Another step is to transform all women into victims; this is easily done by saying that those women who suffered violence did so *because* they were women. This makes their sex the cause of the violence, which is, therefore, directed at all women. A third step is to define all people falling outside this charmed circle of official victimhood as real or potential aggressors. This makes violence

THE ROAD TO EQUITY

done to men less worthy of condemnation and even occasionally worthy of praise because they are members of the group guilty of inflicting all violence and, therefore, deserving of punishment. Suddenly we find ourselves in a dimly lit ethical bog fraught with danger. If violence done to any individual is not treated with the same seriousness and deemed as great a moral evil as violence done to any other, some other enterprise than the rejection of violence is at work.

Opposing Numbers

OUR MENTAL REFLEXES are now so conditioned that it is hard to conceive the notion that violence against women may not be the major social problem presented by violence today. It might be revealing, therefore, to try a little exercise in imagination. What would happen if we reversed the assumptions of the present campaign against male violence against women? Could we make the same sort of partial reading of the facts as the ideologues, but with men painted as the victims? Could we take every statistical difference between men and women and portray them as evidence of systemic discrimination against men? It is surprisingly easy to do. The purpose, however, would be only to show how shallow the groupthink approach is to the complex and subtle question of violence, and how dehumanizing it is to every actor in this human drama. For brevity's sake I am going to refer to this general pattern of explanation of violence as the "sex-is-it" explanation, partly because sex is taken here as the key factor explaining patterns of violence, but also because the term has the advantage of being very close to "sexist." This is precisely what the sex-is-it account is.*

---

* It will be necessary in this section to refer to a great number of statistics, academic studies, and other works. While wishing to avoid footnotes, I know that many readers will want to be able to verify the facts cited. My compromise is to give a reference for each statistic or direct quotation and to complement that with a list of easily obtained books and articles at the end of the essay for further reading.

Our exercise in imagination might begin with the portrayal of men as legitimate objects of violence. Men are constantly singled out as objects of violence, so much so that there is a widespread belief among men that it is shameful and humiliating to complain about such violence. Many men feel themselves to be weak and despicable if they are incapable of defending themselves from physical attack.

Paradoxically, this attitude seems to be shared by many advocates of women's rights. In their 1987 study of battered wives, *Battered But Not Beaten*, the Canadian Advisory Council on the Status of Women (CACSW) deplored the fact that when the problem of wife battering was first raised officially in the House of Commons in 1980, the response of many (male) MPs was to laugh. This may have betrayed a callous indifference to the problem. But almost all of us, and certainly many women's groups, routinely refuse to entertain as anything but a joke and a red herring the problem of husband battering. There is a refusal to consider that violence against men may be the result of "systemic factors," while it is apparently obvious that violence against women can only be explained this way. As the CACSW's report says, violence by wives against husbands should be taken "very seriously," but it should be dealt with "on an individual basis" — an obvious refusal to come to grips with its systemic nature.

The humour in the image of husband battering comes from two sources. The first is precisely this deeply rooted prejudice that men's problems are individual, and if their wives beat them, they had better learn to defend themselves. Second, it comes from the matronizing assumption that every husband is Mike Tyson or Arnold Schwarzenegger, while every wife is Blondie Bumstead or Sally Field. Of course, in most cases, a punch from a man does more damage than one from a woman; on the other hand, approximately one-third of people murdered by their spouse in any one year in Canada are men, suggesting that physical damage from women can be severe. In the USA in 1984, 43% of spousal homicide victims were husbands (Steinmetz & Lucca, 1988) and studies covering a longer period indicate that victims of cross-sex spousal homicides are equally divided between men and women (Curtis, 1974; Steinmetz & Lucca, 1988). A different study of 6,200 cases of domestic assault reported to the U.S. National Crime Survey concluded that "violence against men is much more destructive than violence against women . . . Male victims are injured more often and more seriously than are female victims" (McLeod, 1984). Other studies of violent crime in Canada (Hatch & Faith, 1985; Johnson, 1986) showed that a *higher* proportion of the victims of female attackers were injured during the crime than when a man was the assailant, and women were almost as likely as men to use a weapon in such assaults. Finally, an American study of the available literature documenting aggression found that "61% of all studies reviewed did not show men to be more aggressive than women," and that women did not show "consistently lower tendencies than men to be physically aggressive" (McNeely & Robinson-Simpson, 1987).

In any case, at least with respect to domestic violence, the official definition of wife battering is so much larger than this as to make the question of relative physical strength almost beside the point. Here is how the CACSW defines such battering:

> the loss of dignity, control, and safety as well as the feeling of power-lessness and entrapment experienced by women who are the direct victims of ongoing or repeated physical, psychological, economic, sexual and/or verbal violence or who are subjected to persistent threats or the witnessing of such violence against their children, other relatives, friends, pets and/or cherished possessions. . . . The term . . . will also be understood to encompass the ramifications of the violence for the woman, her children, her friends and relatives and for society as a whole.

It is certainly fair to argue that poverty makes the effects of violence harder to deal with, and in identifying the aggravating effects of poverty on battered women, groups like the CACSW are on sound ground. Again, however, this would require them, if their commitment was really to reduce the ill effects of violence as such, to concentrate on the real explanatory factors of violence, and to abandon their mistaken and contentious concentration on sex. Poor men, after all, are far more likely statistically to be victims of violence than rich women. Furthermore, while lobby groups often claim that the economic dependence of women on abusive husbands makes them more vulnerable, in fact, low-income women, at least in the U.S., "are more likely than affluent women to leave domestic arrangements involving spouse abuse" (McNeely & Robinson-Simpson, 1987).

Continuing the sex-is-it analysis of violence, one familiar index of the way violence against men is encouraged and legitimized is through the media. If we were to equalize the number of graphic displays of the violent deaths of men and women on television and in films, according to one study, literally two hundred times more women would have to be shown to die on screens across the land (Farrell, 1986). Another survey, this time of 1,000 randomly chosen advertisements (Hayward, 1989), showed these conclusions: in the portrayal of male-female couples "100 percent of the ignorant ones were male. 100 percent of those who lost a contest . . . who smelled bad . . . who were put down . . . were male. 100 percent of the objects of rejection . . . of anger . . . of violence were male." In fact, the earlier study of film and television (Farrell, 1986), extended now to the portrayal of violence in cartoon strips, confirmed the earlier findings, and also found only one taboo, one image of violence vis-à-vis the two sexes that was never displayed: female-female violence. So while it is undeniable that the perpetrators of violence against women in the media are almost exclusively men, violence done by men to other men is overwhelmingly more frequent.

Women, on the other hand, while often portrayed as the victims of violence, are hardly ever portrayed as its perpetrators. This, too, distorts the facts. In 1985, for instance, nearly 7,000 women (versus about 60,000 men) were charged with violent offences under the Criminal Code (Johnson in Adelberg & Currie, 1987), and their share of all crimes is rising relative to men. Such violence, while not as obvious as that started by men, is clearly a reality. Perhaps the film *Thelma and Louise* represents a liberating breakthrough for women in that it is now acceptable to portray them as performing violence — as long as men are the victims. This suggests, and the statistics confirm, that men are seen as fair game for violence by both men and women, and, therefore, their potential and actual aggressors are far greater in number.

With respect to domestic violence, Dr. Susanne Steinmetz, who has made an extensive study of the topic, has cited more than 40 different studies regarding spousal abuse. According to her analysis, "These studies tended toward the same conclusion: that among abusive relationships, about 50% of the time the abuse was mutual, about 25% of the time the woman only was abused, and about 25% of the time the man only was abused . . . women are as likely as men to initiate violence against a partner without retaliation" (quoted in Brown, 1992). In a cross-cultural study of six countries (including Canada), Steinmetz found that in each society "the percentage of husbands who used violence was similar to the percentage of violent wives" (Steinmetz & Lucca, 1988).

A recent Canadian study went even further. After having established that their work suggested that about "4 in 10 women who are married or cohabiting engage in some form of abuse tactic as a mode of conflict resolution," Reena Sommer and her colleagues at the University of Manitoba went on to point out that "the overall rates of violence among females reported in this study are higher than those reported for males in other studies examining the prevalence of abuse between intimate partners" (Sommer, et al., 1992). It is also helpful to note, in passing, that it would be quite wrong to leap to the conclusion that the women's violence detailed here could be explained in terms of self-defence. American studies have demonstrated that women initiate violence just as often as men do (Straus, 1989). Nor is this violence somehow the special product of male-female relations: violence between partners in lesbian relationships is statistically just as prevalent as in unions between men and women, and higher than in male homosexual couples (Waterman, et al., 1989); when women criminally assault someone, three times out of four it is another woman (Hatch & Faith, 1985), whereas only a third of men's victims are women. Women are much more frequently the ones to commit elder and child abuse (McNeely, 1983; Steinmetz & Lucca, 1988), and in cases of criminal assault are twice as likely as men to assault acquaintances and three times as likely to assault relatives. According to Holly Johnson (1986), female attackers are known or related to their victims in 65% of cases, while this is true of only 30% of male offenders. One of the principal reasons given by abused husbands as to why they did not leave the abusive relationship is that they "are afraid to leave for fear that further violence would be directed toward the children. Recognizing that men are not likely to receive custody of the children . . . men feel that by staying they are providing some protection for their children" (Steinmetz & Lucca, 1988).

Approaching our subject from another angle, given the fact of human violence, women are protected by many prevailing social attitudes, including those much-despised ones of chivalry, honour, and fair play. In spite of the much greater intimacy of their individual relations with women — and, therefore, the greater number of occasions in which violence could be used — men are far more likely to use violence with each other than against women.

Social attitudes, taken in the round, are at least as plausibly restraining of violence against women as encouraging of it. But beyond that those same attitudes are far more tolerant of violence performed by women than by men. Study after study of the justice and sentencing system has shown that men habitually are meted out stiffer penalties than women for the same violent crimes performed under similar circumstances (Johnston, et al., 1987). An American legal observer, commenting on the use of the "battered wife syndrome" as a defence by wives who have murdered their husbands, notes that

> by exploiting the traditional stereotypes regarding women's weaknesses and vulnerability, [it] licenses the quick use of deadly force by a specialized group and stands as an ironic contradiction both to the social equality sought by women and to the basic aim of the criminal law . . . bestowing upon the abused wife the unique right to destroy her tormentor at her own discretion. (Rittenmeyer in McNeely & Robinson-Simpson, 1987)

This picture flies in the face of some of our most cherished beliefs about violence and its victims. We have firmly anchored in our minds another picture, one of women as the overwhelming — and blameless — victims of violent crime. Can we be so far off the mark about our own social reality?

The answer is that there is no end to the human capacity for self-deception. One of the reasons for our dependence on statistics and the social sciences to illuminate our self-understandings is that they represent an effort to see beyond our anecdotal experience to spot the underlying patterns — patterns we are only too eager to miss. As for what statistics tell us regarding the incidence of violent crime against women as opposed to men, we must be prudent. Official crime figures are immediately suspect because of uneven reporting levels and perhaps even because of the lack of sympathy of police officers themselves. It is often contended, for example, that women are much less likely to report violent crimes, especially rape. It is unclear, however, that this cuts only one way. Other research evidence shows clearly that men are even more reluctant than women to report crimes of violence of which they are victim, due to ignorance, embarrassment, and other factors. Johnson (1986) reports that the "violent incidents least likely to be reported to police were those involving single female offenders. . . . Victims of female offenders were more likely . . . not to report the incident because it was a personal matter, and out of a wish to protect the offender."

With respect to domestic relations, several studies found that women are more likely than men to seek help from an agency or to call the police (McNeely & Robinson-Simpson, 1987; Steinmetz & Lucca, 1988). And, irony of ironies, some feminists have been willing to use police statistics to demonstrate that husband abuse is rare and, therefore, unimportant. An alternative (and more plausible) explanation is that the social and other pressures on men not to report their victimization are very high. A study (McLeod, 1984) of police files in Detroit, for instance, found that a quarter of recorded assaults on wives were serious enough to be labelled "aggravated," whereas 86% of those on husbands were so labelled (41% of the male victims had to be hospitalized overnight or longer, and nearly all required emergency medical attention, surely indicating that assaults on husbands have to be much more serious, on average, before they will wind up in the legal system (Christensen, 1992).

In addition, the huge political pressure on police forces to show themselves to be tough on violence against women may help account for the recent Statistics Canada study of police reports suggesting that men and women were equally victims of violence (reported in *Globe and Mail*, November 19, 1992). Even Statscan felt compelled to emphasize strongly that these results were widely at variance with most other studies of violence. This qualification, however, was not widely reported in the media.

But there are other ways to get more accurate figures. One is to go out and get a statistically significant number of people of both sexes to talk about their personal experience of violent crime. This is precisely what the Canadian Solicitor-General's department did in its Canadian Urban Victimization Survey in order to obtain a more accurate picture than that offered by official crime statistics.

THE ROAD TO EQUITY

A striking image of violent crime emerged from a huge sample of 61,000 residents of seven major cities in Canada in 1982. Violent crime is exceptionally rare in Canada, the survey showed; four out of five crimes are against property rather than persons. Within the overall crime totals, sexual assault of *either* sex constituted about one-third of one percent; theft with violence constituted exactly one percent; and assault 5.7 percent. And while women were seven times more likely than men to have been victims of sexual assault, men outnumbered women by a good margin in every other category of violent crime. Furthermore, the shame and social stigma attached to being a male victim of sexual assault are such that male victimization is likely systematically understated. We simply don't know because so little research effort is directed at the question of male victims of violence. In spite of this systematic neglect, one thing is clear: whichever way one slices it, men are the principal victims of violent crime in Canada.

The Urban Crime Survey's authors make a point of noting that the generalized fear on the part of women in Canada of sexual assault cannot be explained by the actual rates of such attacks, which in their extreme form are relatively rare. This sentiment is echoed by Statscan researcher Holly Johnson, who says, "One of the ironies of crime in Canada is that those who express the greatest fear of crime are often the least victimized. While women and elderly people are the most likely to fear for their personal safety, they are not the groups at highest risk of victimization" (quoted in Brown, 1992).

In 1990, a Statistics Canada survey of 9,870 people revealed a similar picture: it found that the principal victims of crime were men, the young, city dwellers, people living alone, students, and the unemployed. Those surveyed reported too few cases of sexual assault to allow any statistically significant estimates of its prevalence to be made for the population as a whole. In the same year, the Department of Justice published its annual evaluation of sexual-assault legislation in Canada. There, one can read that over

19

the period 1977–88, a total of 201,972 cases of sexual aggression were reported (of which on average 15% would prove unfounded). This means that over twelve years about 0.75% of the population would report being a victim of such a crime.

One of the things these figures demonstrate — bearing in mind that this is an exercise in sex-is-it imagination — is that men are disadvantaged by their socialization (their "gender"), which teaches them that they must bear suffering and pain stoically and show no fear in the face of danger. They are also taught that they must solve their problems through individual action, so they are unlikely to appeal to official agencies for protection. The fact that most police are men compounds the problem, because it is humiliating for a man to have to admit his inability to protect himself to another man, especially a stranger.

On top of this, men *and* women are taught to believe that women are weak and frequently victimized, so that protective resources should disproportionately be directed to women. Men, therefore, participate in their own abuse and oppression by accepting society's false portrayal of the relative victimization of men and women. And the violence against men *is* systemic (if one believes in the standard yardsticks of proof for "systemic" abuse): one survey of available research showed that "men are between three and four times more likely to commit suicide . . . two and three times as likely to be murdered; women live longer, enjoy better health and are less prone to insanity, alcoholism, drug abuse and crime" (Brown, 1992).

Again the media participate in the systematic distortion of the relative effects of violent crime on different segments of the population, exaggerating the effects on women and downplaying those on men. This is because the media are interested in crimes (and victims) that have the greatest human interest. These, however, are precisely those in which the victim is most atypical. A story about a violent attack on a middle-aged white woman is just more interesting to many people than one about an attack on a poor

Filipino or Haitian immigrant man or an unemployed (male) coal miner, even though the latter is statistically far more likely to occur. This little workout of the muscles of the imagination is certain to raise hackles. It needs to be said, however, that one of the signs that our mental pictures of violence are often not based on demonstrable fact, but on fact-resistant faith, is the unreasoning reaction to arguments that question those images. Many of the statistical arguments against the prevailing belief in men as the exclusive perpetrators and women as the innocent victims of violence are rejected out of hand as suspect science or malevolent male denial, while in contrast every study and statistic that supports this belief becomes an unassailable truth. In one example of this intellectual slipperiness, the CACSW's study, referred to earlier, briefly considered the problem of "husband battering." They concluded that those women who were identified in the study as batterers "assumed the traditionally dominant male role in their relationships." In other words, by the fact of their violence, these women became honorary men. The men in the relationship, one supposes, became honorary women by virtue of being victims. In other words, in the teeth of the evidence, the problem to be understood remains male violence against women.

One refuge to which the partisans of this argument will probably retreat is "socially constructed gender roles." This impressive-sounding phrase is meant to signal the undeniable fact that the society in which we are brought up influences what we think it means to be a man or a woman. What is at issue in discussions about violence, for example, is not how men and women relate in the abstract, but how people relate when living up to our (Western, patriarchal, capitalist) set of social expectations about sex roles. Any person who occupies the male role will be predisposed to be violent toward any person playing the female role, whatever the sex of the respective role players. This escape route will not do, for no social role is played in a vacuum. Socialization into roles is a powerful tool in understanding human behaviour, but we all inhabit a thousand roles that meet and mingle and influence one another in mysterious ways. Personality is in part the intersection of all the roles a person plays. To raise the question of social roles is thus to take seriously the idea that to understand what any particular individual does, we have to look at him or her as an individual. We cannot make assumptions about a person on the basis of such superficial similarities as sex or a single shared social role.

Allow me to launch an illustrative counterstrike in anticipation of how the arguments I am reporting will be handled by the faithful. Take one of the foundation stones of the belief that Canadian men are merely violent attacks waiting to happen. Everyone has heard the statistic cited at the beginning of this essay: one million battered women in Canada. Where does this statistic come from? It can be traced back to the same 1987 report for the Advisory Council on the Status of Women entitled *Battered But Not Beaten*. There, the author, Linda MacLeod, indicates that her intention was to correct the impression left by a rough 1980 estimate she had done that one in ten Canadian women was battered by her partner. An estimate this time, MacLeod said, could "lead to an oversimplification of the problem, a continued blurring of the complexities so important to our future progress in this area." Ironically, she then goes on to make just such an estimate, the only aspect of her study that has remained in the public mind. How did she get her one million figure? The method is instructive.

Starting with the 110 shelters for battered women that were able to provide figures in 1985, MacLeod notes that they admitted 15,730 women explicitly because they were "physically, psychologically or sexually abused by their husbands or partners." These statistics are extrapolated to the then existing 230 such centres across the country, to produce a figure of 33,000 women admitted because they were battered. "On average," each shelter had to turn down one of every two requests for accommodation, so the figure is doubled to 65,000. Attention then shifts to an unrelated study done in London, Ontario, that suggests that 89% of battered women in that city did not seek emergency shelter, so we multiply our figure by nine to get 600,000. Then, on the basis of a "guess-timate" that only two out of three women report battering to an official agency, we add 300,000. And then, with no explanation at all, this 900,000 is simply rounded off to one million.

From a statistical point of view, there are several steps here that render the final figure meaningless and of little scientific value. The final rounding off of 100,000 alone, for instance, is given no explicit justification, but represents literally more than seven times the original hard figure of 15,730, which was the point of departure. But perhaps the most eloquent proof of the unfounded nature of the one million claim comes from journalist and former Université de Québec à Montréal (UQAM) professor Roch Côté. Côté (1990) applied this statistical method to the figures available in Quebec for 1990, and came to the conclusion that there were 2.7 million battered women over eighteen in the province. Unfortunately, census figures show that there were only 2,542,040 women over eighteen in Quebec in 1986.

My argument so far has been twofold: violence against women has become a politicized issue, so that the way we gather information about and discuss such violence has been distorted; and we neglect violence as an issue with grave consequences for many *men*, as well as women.

At the end of 1993, Statscan published the results of the first ever "Violence Against Women Survey," an apparently damning indictment of male violence in this country. A full analysis of the survey is not possible here, but it is worth a moment's examination as an example of the sort of politicization of this field just referred to. Take the question of what kind of incidents of violence are studied in the report. Much is made of the fact that only behaviours considered an offence under the Canadian Criminal Code are dealt with. Many people assume that behaviours that could result in charges under the Criminal Code must by their nature be extremely serious and especially damaging to the victim. In fact, there are many behaviours that theoretically could serve as grounds for a criminal charge, where both victim and objective observers would find this response out of all proportion to the offence. Violence, crime, and victimhood are not purely objective phenomena, but depend, too, on how the people involved *feel* about what has happened. Leave out this reality, and a simple question about whether one has ever been the victim of actions that *could* be considered an offence will produce a wholly misleading response.

In order to get more impressive numbers, the kind that attract the attention of the media and policy-makers, sensational and misleading names are attached to incidents that *the victims themselves* report as having been without physical or emotional consequences. Such manipulation of the figures can only result in the trivialization of those incidents with real and lasting harmful results for their victims, as well as serving to increase the belief that violence against women is a generalized fact among men. Many victims makes for many aggressors.

I noted earlier that the other problem with the way we discuss violence against women is that we neglect violence as an issue with grave consequences for many *men,* as well as women. Here, too, the Statscan study contributes to the problem, not to the solution. On this score, there is little I can add to the pertinent observations of Diane LeBlanc, a columnist in the Halifax *Chronicle-Herald,* following the report's release:

> In order to fairly and rightly comment on male violence against women, we should be able to weigh this study's results with the findings of polls that ask exactly the same questions about male or female violence against men. . . . Women's groups, politicians, statisticians and the media are doing us all a disservice by painting so skewed a vision.

IF THE EVIDENCE IS, to put it charitably, so ambiguous about the sex-is-it explanation of violence, what accounts for its continued wide currency? Two possible explanations spring immediately to mind. The first is that the one-sided condemnation of violence against women (or, even more fashionably, of male violence) instead of violence per se, is the result of an assumption that men deserve to be the objects of violence. There might be found here an easy but indefensible logical slide from one undeniable truth to an unjustified conclusion. The undeniable truth is that *some* men are the authors of the great majority of violence in the world. The unjustified conclusion is to generalize the guilt of a few to a whole group that are superficially like them, that is to say, to all men. All men are guilty by hormonal association, they are, therefore, all fair game, and it is only just that they suffer violence, for don't the morally guilty deserve punishment? To the extent that this view exists, it constitutes an attitude to be deplored by all those for whom violence as such is the crime.

Even more interesting and suggestive is the second explanation of the unequal condemnations of violence against the two sexes, and it is the mirror image of the first. This explanation holds that women uniquely deserve not to be the victims of violence, that all women are innocent by hormonal association and, therefore, that no women bear any responsibility for violence. But this is clearly misguided. Leave aside for a moment the wrongheadedness of the sex-is-it, as opposed to the individual, approach to understanding violence and its origins. By the standard of group responsibility, women are guilty of a large proportion of violence in society; their hands are dirty, too, as many of the studies cited earlier show.

If we were really interested in determining the causes of violence because we wanted to protect the integrity of individuals, this distribution of responsibility among individuals would be important because it tells us where to direct our efforts to defeat violence. But if one listens to the rhetoric surrounding this issue, it seems that such efforts are not important. Could that be because violence is not actually the point?

The point may just be that there is an advantage in being thought of as a victim. The philosopher Bertrand Russell was surely on the mark when he referred to the "myth of the moral superiority of the oppressed." It is a myth — albeit a powerful and durable one — that victims are, by their very victimization, rendered morally innocent. And innocence is an important instrument of *power*. Victimhood is powerful. As the black author and English professor Shelby Steele put it in *The Content of Our Character,*

> the human animal almost never pursues power without first convincing himself that he is *entitled* to it. And this feeling of entitlement has its own precondition: to be entitled, one must first believe in one's own innocence, at least in the area where one wants to feel entitled. By innocence, I mean a feeling of essential goodness in relation to others and, therefore, a feeling of superiority over others. Our innocence always inflates us and deflates those we seek power over. Once inflated, we are entitled; we are in fact licensed to go after the power our innocence tells us we deserve. In this sense, *innocence is power.* (5)

This, of course, contradicts the ideologue's conception of power. For the ideologue, power always flows from structures or systems or institutions. It is the crude, brute power of interests backed up by force. A police force beating up striking miners, or the courts forcing women to act like the property of their husbands — now *that's* power.

No one can deny that such power exists. What is remarkable, however, is just how ineffective it is. The crudest brute force of the Soviet army and security forces could not overpower the populace once the Soviet state was seen to be vulnerable. Ditto for the Shah of Iran before the Islamic revolution. Power relations are always relations of mutual dependence; they are never a one-way street. And in the long run, power flows from moral relations and beliefs far more effectively than from the barrel of a gun.

The ideologues deny this, in theory. Actions flow from interests, the interests I have as a man, or as a capitalist, interests that by definition are opposed to those of the group in whose embrace I am locked in the dance of the dialectic. Change only comes, the theory runs, when the Outs seize real power and then use coercion to force change on the Ins. In practice, of course, it is quite different. In practice, feminist ideologues in particular use a carefully crafted moral structure of female innocence and male guilt to bring about change. How does this work?

Most of us want to act in accordance with our deepest beliefs. Most of us also are prone to rationalizing, to ignoring or downplaying inconvenient facts so that we can square our desires with our morals by not entirely thinking through the consequences of what we do. But a moral code that never conflicts with what we desire isn't worth its salt. Only when such conflicts arise do we take the moral measure of a man or a woman. In such cases if we choose deep moral commitment over desire, we are exalted. If desire overrides our better selves, we are shamed and lose face with ourselves and others. Lord Jim, in the eponymous novel by Joseph Conrad, could only expiate one egregious dereliction of duty by the ultimate sacrifice. Every day, millions of men and women atone for millions of less spectacular transgressions through quiet acts of individual moral strength. We must redeem our failures to meet our own standards; that is part of the wholesome role of guilt in morality. By expiation we hope to recover our lost innocence, the state in which there is no separation between what is and what ought to be.

To appeal to the standards by which we profess to live, and to point out inconsistencies between these standards and our actions, is to take ourselves seriously as individuals with judgement and moral strength, and to assume we have the character necessary to correct any backsliding that our inconsistencies may reveal. Guilt is powerful because it gets directly inside our head. We are compelled to honour our standards of fairness or decency or honour or justice, or else lose face in our own eyes, as well as those of others.

To understand *real* power, sociologist Randall Collins has argued, one must understand that "both rewards and coercion are relatively weak forms of control. If you want to get something done reasonably well, you have to find a way *to make people want to do it*" (my emphasis). Guilt fits the bill perfectly, because most of us want to believe that we are both honourable in action and consistent in belief. We are stung and motivated to change when confronted with proof of the opposite. We are prepared to make sacrifices to make honest — and innocent — people of ourselves once again.

But it is tempting to use guilt to manipulate human behaviour, especially in the context of relations between men and women. A little logical and statistical legerdemain and a whole class of the population — men — can be made to feel guilty for a whole series of atrocious crimes of violence against women, which individually the vast majority of men would never commit. To expiate those sins, all sorts of transfers of resources, money, jobs, education, and social programs become necessary, ostensibly compensating women.

Even more important, a powerful psychology of collective solidarity is created and becomes self-perpetuating. Every time there is an act of violence by a man against a woman it reaffirms the belief that men as a group are attacking women as a group. Ritual ties and emotional bonds unite the members of the group who can cleanse themselves of any responsibility for violence by projecting it onto the conveniently identified guilty party. The particular details of any incident, like the Montreal massacre, become unimportant because the people involved are outside the ritual; they are merely its occasion, not its participants. They furnish the fuel of the solidarity-producing machine, and when this fuel is consumed the only lasting residue is a consciousness of the sex of victim and aggressor. Of the individual lives, beliefs, and decisions that alone can furnish the true explanation of what happened, there remains not a trace.

        WHAT IS PERHAPS LESS OBVIOUS than the advantages of the guilt gambit are its costs. These are three: a misidentification of the problem and, therefore, a misunderstanding of the solutions; a long-term undermining of the moral system on which guilt rests; and, most importantly perhaps, the freezing of both women and men in relative postures of attack and self-defence. These costs should be examined in more detail.

1. Misidentification of the problem

The misidentification of the problem to which I am referring, of course, is the belief that men as a group are the cause of violence against women as a group, and that this is the only kind of violence that really matters.

To say that every man must confront the rapist or Marc Lépine inside him is as superficial and unhelpful as saying that every woman must confront the nymphomaniac or Lizzie Borden inside her. Possession of an axe does not make one an axe murderer, although it is undeniable that one needs an axe to be one. No more does mere possession of a penis make one a rapist. Instrument is not a synonym for intent. To think otherwise is to commit the cardinal sin of believing that biology is destiny.

Each person has the physical equipment to commit moral atrocities, to be Marc Lépine or Lizzie Borden. But each of us also has the same physical capacity to perform moral heroism, to be Mother Teresa or Saint Francis of Assisi. What most of us lack is the strength of character, the moral capacity for great good or great evil. In other words, the basic theory of the feminist account of violence is wrong. And if the account is wrong, then the solutions it proposes will be largely ineffective.

We are all familiar with similar explanations of the goings-on around us that similarly have been proved mistaken. Take what Randall Collins calls the "broken-family-and-blighted-neighbourhood hypothesis about crime." Our commonsense view is that broken homes, stress, deprivation, and poverty lead to crime. But the facts don't fit our commonsense view. Not every child of divorce becomes a delinquent, no more than every poor person or member of racial minorities becomes a criminal. Some rich white people commit crimes, as do some poor black people, but most in either group do not.

If, then, some women are violent but most aren't, and if more men are violent but most aren't, and if both women and men are victims of violence but men in considerably larger proportions than women, then we need considerably more complex and nuanced understandings of violence as a social fact. Only then will we direct our efforts to true causes, and not go hunting witches or, more appropriately in this instance, warlocks.

2. *Long-term decline of the moral basis of guilt*

The second cost of the guilt strategy in regard to violence is a long-term undermining of the morality on which guilt rests. To be successful, the assignation of collective guilt to a group depends on the receptiveness of its individual members. That receptiveness, in turn, depends, first, on each individual's belief that he or she bears a part of the responsibility and, second, on the belief that individual action can absolve them of the guilt. The importance of this sense of personal efficacy cannot be exaggerated.

Let us suppose that the first condition is fulfilled, for men can hardly deny that most violence against men and women is committed by men. Let us also suppose that the second condition is by and large now met, and that a great many men of goodwill are, in their private lives and in their political and business decisions, working to root out attitudes and behaviours that might lead to violence against women. Can the two conditions continue to be satisfied in the long run?

Remember that while the practice of the sex-is-it campaign is to appeal to individual guilt and, therefore, individual responsibility and efficacy, its theory — its explicit justification — is quite different. The theory is that violence against women is systemic, and consciously or unconsciously performed, promoted, and condoned by all men through institutions and systems of their design that serve their interests. The result is that while men's moral sensibilities are constantly appealed to, men are also constantly told that no matter what they may believe they are doing, be it ever so peaceful and constructive, they are, in fact, individually and collectively contributing to the problem. Every act of violence by a man against a women is seized on as further evidence of the systemic nature of the problem, therefore placing it beyond the reach of the possibility of individual atonement.

Like Joseph K. in Kafka's surrealistic trial, most men are thus confronted with an impossible moral conundrum. They are constantly assured of their guilt, but the charge is a vague and generalized one. In spite of their most strenuous introspection, they cannot find it in their hearts to accept that they are, in fact, responsible for all the transgressions supposedly recorded on their moral balance sheet. No matter what they *do*, they are guilty, and no matter what penance they perform, they can never redeem themselves. Only the most saintly among men, then, will agree to endure the regimen of sterile self-flagellation to which they are invited. What always surprises me is the number of candidates for sainthood.

When their best (but fallible and limited) efforts are constantly dismissed as unimportant and as carrying no hope of a solution to the problem of violence, men cease believing in their own efficacy as individuals. If it is a systemic problem, then only systemic approaches will solve it. The best among the male population queue up, confused, for sainthood, while the worst say, "Thank God for that, now I'm off the hook."

If I'm right that the sex-is-it explanation of violence against women is fundamentally mistaken, even greater efforts to attack this pseudo-problem systemically will fail. This will produce even more clamorous denunciations of men who refuse to "relinquish power" and to "stop abusing women," so that this road, too, will appear hopeless. The likely result will simply be a tossing up of hands and a growing belief in the intractable nature of the problem. This undermines the guilt reflex because in the long run no one can be made to feel guilty for what they honestly believe is quite beyond their power to influence.

3. *Needless animosity between men and women*

The third cost of the guilt strategy is the needless animosity it generates between those who must cooperate if the very real problem of violence is to be dealt with effectively: men and women.

To make the best use of guilt, one must be innocent. The real power of guilt comes from different relative levels of guilt and innocence; thus the power that the sex-is-it account confers on women. But no human being is entirely innocent. Popes and television evangelists are only two of the groups that have tried to assume this mantle, only to be shown to have feet of clay like the rest of us. It is a normal human reflex of skepticism to want to probe a claim to power made on the basis of such an exceedingly difficult ground as innocence.

We all know that the best defence is a strong offence. The best defence against the questioning of one's innocence is thus constantly to raise the level of guilt that others are made to feel. I have lost count of the number of times I have been told that my skepticism regarding the sex-is-it account of violence is not only evidence of my denial of personal responsibility as a man for violence against women, but is also part of a larger "backlash" by men who refuse to hear the truths of feminism.

The costs of these charges are obvious. There is no more sterile activity than the laying of blame and the necessary search for the guilty that it brings in its train. For the believers in sex-is-it, the need to lay blame creates a psychology of self-vindication, in which one's moral superiority is assured by every bit of new evidence of the vileness of men. The great and good, the *bien pensants,* the morally superior of every society, have always enjoyed quivers of pleasure at the baseness and degradation of their inferiors: "There but for the grace of God go I." Hypocrisy and double standards are the inevitable result. Because the satisfaction that this gives can only be maintained through the belief in the inferiority of the "other," finding the cause of the vile behaviour in the other must be avoided, as must any recognition of the essential sameness of self and other. The real goal is self-justification, which requires that the problem continue.

The moral rectitude of those who cannot accept sex-is-it explanations must, therefore, constantly be attacked, both to keep their natural skepticism in check, as well as to maintain the pecking order of smugness. Guilt attacks are most effective when the object already believes in his own guilt and, therefore, finds them justified. But when the object of the attack feels strongly that he's being made to shoulder a disproportionate share of responsibility, the dynamic changes. It then appears that a wholesome appeal to an honest reflex is being manipulated, not to solve a problem, but to cause unnecessary pain. This changes the dynamic of guilt described earlier.

Guilt hurts. A certain behaviour is demanded, or pain will be applied. The difference, however, is that when one believes one's guilt reflex is being used as a weapon, the pain one feels is seen as an attack, not something that comes from within. What we know about pain as a way of obtaining desired behaviour is that it is about the least effective method imaginable. Studies in motivational psychology show clearly that pain does not, in the first instance, make people want to do what their tormentor desires. Pain makes people angry and fearful, and it makes them want to escape; it also makes them want to retaliate against their tormentors. It makes people sullen, uncooperative and, in appearance at least, stupid. These are all attitudes characteristic of people seeking to defend themselves from attack. That is why when one seeks the cooperation of another in the creative solution of a problem, it is not advisable to attack them. Far better to make them part of the solution than the incorrigible and blameworthy source of the problem.

AT THE END OF THE DAY, we are all victims, because we live in a society in which violence harms people and denies their equal worth, and because violence, however regrettable, must be a part of civilized life, through police, jails, armies, and the like. We are all guilty because we all harbour attitudes that can sometimes lead to violence. Nathalie Provost, one of the survivors of Marc Lépine's attack, showed great moral courage in accepting this about herself in the film about her. She observed: "Sometimes I, too, can't take it anymore, and I blame it on others. We all have a bit of Marc Lépine inside us, we all have those moments when we can no longer tolerate what is different, can no longer tolerate people who don't do what we expect them to do."

Some people — I like to think most — who use violence do so because it appears to them their only option in the tangled skein of intentions, hopes, circumstances, and obstacles in which they live. Some people use violence because they are bad and perhaps evil. Some people use violence because it is their job. Some violence may be eliminated through the provision of new options — economic, emotional, sexual, or others. But some will remain, and the best we can do is to try to guard against it and to punish offenders.

Pitting one group composed of the more or less guilty against another will do nothing to diminish violence, and may complicate the problem further. The question we have to face above all else, then, is do we actually want to solve the problem of violence against *anyone*, or are we embroiled in a symbolic struggle for moral superiority whose logic requires that violence continue? The evidence, I fear, is in favour of the latter.

FURTHER READING

Brinkerhoff, M.B. and E. Lupri. "Interspousal Violence." *Canadian Journal of Sociology* 13 (4): 407–34.

Brickman, Julie and John Briere. "Incidence of Rape and Sexual Assault in an Urban Canadian Population." *International Journal of Women's Studies* 7 (3): 195–206.

Brown, Grant. *The Employment Equity Empress Has No Clothes.* Edmonton: Gender Issues Education Foundation, 1992.

Christensen, Ferrel. *Balancing the Approach to Spouse Abuse.* Calgary: Wordsmith Works, 1992.

Collins, Randall. *Sociological Insight: An Introduction to Non-Obvious Sociology.* New York: Oxford University Press, 1982.

Côté, Roch. *Manifeste d'un Salaud.* Montréal: Editions du Portique, 1990.

Curtis, L.A. *Criminal Violence.* Lexington: Lexington Books, 1974.

Eisenberg, Nancy and Randy Lennon. "Sex Differences in Empathy and Related Capacities." *Psychological Bulletin* 94 (1983): 100–131.

Elshtain, Jean B. *Women and War.* New York: Basic Books, 1987.

Farrell, Warren. *Why Men Are the Way They Are.* New York: Berkeley Books, 1986.

Fox-Genovese, Elizabeth. "Androcrats Go Home." *The New York Times Review of Books,* October 4, 1987: 32.

Frodi, A., *et al.* "Are Women Always Less Aggressive than Men? A Review of the Experimental Literature." *Psychological Bulletin* 84 (1977).

Gaguin, D. "Spouse Abuse: Data from the National Crime Survey." *Victimology* 2 (1977–8).

Gelles, R.J. and M.A. Strauss. *Intimate Violence: The Causes and Consequences of Abuse in the American Family.* New York: Touchstone Books, 1988.

Greeno, Catherine G. and Eleanor Maccoby. "How Different is the 'Different Voice'?" *Signs* 11 (1986): 310–16.

Hatch, Alison and Karlene Faith. "The Female Offender in Canada." A paper presented at the Annual Meeting of the American Society of Criminology, San Diego, Calif., 13–17 November 1985.

Johnson, Holly. *Women and Crime in Canada.* Ottawa: Solicitor General of Canada, 1986.

———— "Getting the Facts Straight: A Statistical Overview." *Too Few to Count: Canadian Women in Conflict With the Law.* Ellen Adelberg and Claudia Currie, eds. Vancouver: Press Gang, 1987.

Johnston, Janet B., Thomas Kennedy, and Gayle Shuman. "Gender

Differences in Sentencing of Felony Offenders." *Federal Probation 5* (1): 49–55.

Lott, Bernice. "Dual Natures or Learned Behaviour: The Challenge to Feminist Psychology." *Making a Difference: Psychology and the Construction of Gender.* R.T. Hare-Mustin and J. Maracek, eds. New Haven: Yale University Press, 1987.

MacLeod, Linda. *Battered But Not Beaten: Preventing Wife Battering in Canada.* Ottawa: Canadian Advisory Council on the Status of Women, 1987.

McLeod, M. *Domestic Violence: The Measurement Dilemma.* Albany, N.Y.: Hindelang Criminal Justice Research Center, State University of New York, 1982.

——— "Women Against Men: An Examination of Domestic Violence." *Justice Quarterly* 1 (1984), 171–93.

McNeely, R.L. "Race, Sex and Victimization of the Elderly." *Aging in Minority Groups.* McNeely and J.N. Colen eds., Beverly Hills: Sage Publications, 1983.

McNeely, R.L. and Gloria Robinson-Simpson. "The Truth about Domestic Violence: A Falsely Framed Issue." *Social Work* Nov.-Dec. 1987: 485–90.

Mednick, Martha T. "On the Politics of Psychological Constructs: Stop the Bandwagon, I want to Get Off." *American Psychologist* 44 (1989): 1118–23.

Oswald, I. "Domestic Violence by Women." *The Lancet* December 1980: 1253.

Rittenmeyer, S.D. "Of Battered Wives, Self-Defense and Double Standards of Justice." *Journal of Criminal Justice* 9 (1981): 389–95.

Saunders, D.G. "When Battered Women Use Violence: Husband Abuse or Self-Defense?" *Victims and Violence* 1 (1986): 47–60.

Simon, R.J. "American Women and Crime." *Annals of the American Academy of Political and Social Science* 423 (1976): 31–46.

Solicitor General Canada. *National Urban Crime Survey.* Ottawa, 1982.

Sommer, Reena, *et al.* "Alcohol Consumption, Alcohol Abuse, Personality and Female Perpetrated Spouse Abuse." *Personal and Individual Differences* 13 (12): 1315–23.

Sommers, Christina. "The Feminist Revelation." *Ethics, Politics and Human Nature.* Ellen Paul, *et al.,* eds. Cambridge: Basil Blackwell, 1991.

Steinmetz, Suzanne K. "Cross Cultural Marital Abuse." *Journal of Sociology and Social Welfare* 8: 404–14.

Steinmetz, Suzanne K. and Joseph Lucca. "Husband Battering." *Handbook of Family Violence.* Vincent Van Hasselt, *et al.,* eds. New York: Plenum Press, 1988.

Straus, M.A. "Assaults by Wives on Husbands: Implications for Primary Prevention of Family Violence." A paper presented to the 1989 meeting of the American Society for Criminology.

Straus, M.A. and R.J Gelles. "Societal Change and Change in Family Violence from 1975 to 1985 as revealed by two National Surveys." *Journal of Marriage and the Family* 48 (1986): 465–79.

Straus, M.A., R.J. Gelles, and Suzanne K. Steinmetz. *Behind Closed Doors: Violence in the American Family.* New York: Anchor/Doubleday, 1980.

Tavris, Carol. *The Mismeasure of Woman.* New York: Simon and Schuster, 1992.

Tavris, Carol and Carole Wade. *The Longest War: Sex Differences in Perspective.* 2nd ed. San Diego: Harcourt, Brace, Jovanovich, 1984.

Thoma, Stephen. "Estimating Gender Differences in the Comprehension and Preference of Moral Issues." *Developmental Review* 6 (1986): 165–80.

U.S. Bureau of the Census. *National Crime Survey.* Washington, 1975.

Walker, L.E. "Social Consequences of Feminism: The Battered Women's Movement." A paper presented at the annual meeting of the American Psychological Association. New York, September 1979.

Waterman, Caroline, *et al.* "Sexual Coercion in Gay Male and Lesbian Relationships: Predictors and Implications for Support Services." *Journal of Sex Research* 26(1).

White, D.M. and R.H. Abel, eds. *The Funnies, and American Idiom.* Glencoe: The Free Press, 1963.

Wolfgang, M. *Patterns in Criminal Homicide.* New York: Wiley, 1958.

The Road to Equity Is
Paved with Good Intentions

O but we dreamed to mend
What ever mischief seemed
To afflict mankind, but now
That winds of winter blow
Learn that we were crack-pated when we dreamed

W.B. Yeats

HAPPINESS, Aristotle once wisely remarked, is frustratingly coy: it cannot be pursued directly. Like a favourite flower, it cannot be made to grow more quickly by pulling on it. Rather, the best we can do is strive to create the conditions in which happiness is likely to flourish. So it is with the ideal society. With nothing but the best of intentions, many great social reformers have wrought social misery and economic disaster on their fellow citizens. Armed with scientific surveys or scientific socialism, they seem to point the way to a brave new world of social justice. The future can be built, we can make it, it doesn't just have to happen to us.

But the future we make in this way too often ends up looking like Novosibirsk than the New Jerusalem, Airstrip One rather than Arcadia. This truth is repugnant to an age and a culture deeply intoxicated with the illusion of its own power to transform the world and itself nearer to its heart's desire. We are all egalitarians now, for instance, and anything that seems to run counter to that fundamental principle will be swept aside as unworthy of a modern and forward-looking people.

Which brings us to two of the great leitmotifs of Canadian public policy today, the two equities: employment equity and pay equity. Apparently the need for these policies follows from certain facts as the night follows the day. Statistics reveal to us that members of certain groups are "underrepresented" in the workforce, especially at certain levels and in certain professions. Statistics similarly reveal to us a "wage gap" between women's and men's pay. Conclusion: government should force private employers to cease engaging in what is clearly reprehensible discrimination, so that we may truly have a society in which there is equal opportunity, if not equal outcome, in which everyone gets the same crack at everything. Opposition to such measures is not just unkind, but possibly malevolent and certainly self-interested.

Admittedly, it is hard to disagree with the objective of these programs. Take employment equity, for instance, the principal focus here. No need to be a New Democrat to want to nod vigorously in agreement with the Ontario government's description of the problem in its Bill 79 on employment equity, introduced in June 1992:

> Aboriginal people, people with disabilities, members of racial minorities and women . . . experience more discrimination than other people in finding employment, in retaining employment and in being promoted. As a result, they are underrepresented in most areas of employment, especially in senior and management positions.

Similar premises underlie employment equity plans at all levels, such as the federal Employment Equity Act and Contractors Program, provincial policies such as Ontario's, and even municipal plans such as Toronto's. Believing that they have laid bare a pattern of "systemic discrimination," the authors of equity schemes follow up with a list of measures to combat this social evil. In Canada, plans to combat such discrimination usually include an extensive, employer-financed monitoring program of hiring practices and promotion patterns. Bell Canada's quarterly regional employment equity reports are the size of two Toronto telephone directories. It can cost a large company up to $500,000 for a complete review of payroll systems, job classifications, and all job descriptions, which is only the beginning of a complex program, the running of which requires time and resources. In addition, there is room in the government plans for negotiated goals and action plans for the hiring and promotion of these underrepresented groups. In the United States, where such plans have gone the furthest, government-sponsored affirmative action programs have resulted in various detailed and specific quotas and timetables for hiring minorities and women.

Employment equity or affirmative action schemes have been in operation in various countries for several years now, so a lot of evidence is beginning to accumulate about the success of these programs in achieving their stated objectives, and also about the unintended costs and consequences that they have brought in their train. This research tells a story of almost monumental ineptitude and ignorance about economics and justice on the part of government planners. Over and over again, employment equity schemes are shown not to achieve their objectives, because they are based on a misconception about how the employment market works and about discrimination itself. As a result, employment equity and affirmative action have damaged business and competitiveness by driving up costs with little demonstrable benefit in terms of fairness. Perhaps most damning, these same schemes are shown again and again actually to harm the interests of those they are supposed to promote: women, racial minorities, native people, and the disabled.

How is this possible? How can such laudable intentions have gone so wrong? Go back for a moment to the quotation from the

Ontario Employment Equity Act. Most of us are so busy agreeing with its claim that blameworthy discrimination against certain groups exists and ought to be eliminated that we fail to notice the Act's two key ideas about economics and justice.

THE FIRST IDEA IS THAT of "underrepresentation" of certain groups in the workforce, the idea that in a perfectly just world, all groups would be "represented" in every occupation and at every level of responsibility in exact proportion to their share of the population as a whole. The second is that any and all deviation from such a strict "proportional representation" must be a result of present discrimination by employers. Both of these ideas are fallacies, and seeing why is crucial to coming to grips with the evidence concerning the failure of equity policies.

"Proportional representation" assumes, among other things, that the desire and aptitude to perform all tasks is equally distributed throughout the population. This is clearly not so. Germans are concentrated in the brewing industry in America, as are Italians in wine-making in California and British Columbia. There were Yorkshiremen down almost every coal mine in the world for many years, and the chances were great that your watch was made by a Swiss watchmaker and that your parish priest was Irish. Was this discrimination? Hardly. Yorkshiremen, for instance, happened to be born in a county that virtually floats on coal, and generation after generation of miners learned the culture and the practices of coal mining with every breath they drew. In each of these cases, these people were taking advantage of a very simple fact: they came from a region or a culture that exposed them to an intensive knowledge of a particular industry or occupation. The simple fact of a preponderance of people of a certain background in a particular industry cannot be laid at the door of employers; families and whole communities acquire and pass on over generations the knowledge of how to do a job. Parents aspire to see their children follow in their footsteps, and make every effort to see that they succeed in a vocation they know well.

This provides the link to the second fallacy of employment equity: that imbalances in group representation in the workforce must be due to present-day employer discrimination. Cultural traits within different groups can open up certain employment avenues and close others. Thomas Sowell, a black American economist, has noted that 50% of Mexican-American women marry in their teens, whereas only 10% of Japanese-American women do. "It requires little imagination," remarks Sowell, "to see how that must affect opportunities for college attendance and/or lucrative careers quite apart from employer discrimination." Similarly, groups with different cultures place different values on things like education, which has a great long-term impact on career prospects.

A 1990 study by a university sociologist correlating census data on ethnic origins and educational attainments illustrates the astonishingly diverse distribution of these attainments across groups, including visible minority groups, many of whom tie or exceed the educational attainments of Canadians of British origin.

Along a similar vein, Sowell studied the median ages of different American ethnic groups and found a variation ranging from a high of forty-six for Jews to a low of eighteen for Mexican Americans. Analysis of the Canadian data shows a range from almost thirty-five for Jews to a low of just over twenty for aboriginal people. Age representing experience, and experience being a quality for which employers must pay, this age distribution alone accounts for many differences of representation of different groups in different professions and at different levels of responsibility.

Different combinations of age and education within groups also have important consequences for career prospects. It is projected that in the year 2000, 30% of physicians in Canada will be women. Only 10% of all doctors over fifty-five will be women, however, while 43% of those in their thirties will be. Few will deny that this must have some influence on the profile of teachers of medicine at the turn of the century. As a 1990 study for the Association of Canadian Medical Colleges put it, this means that in 2000, "only 13–15% of . . . medically-qualified full professors . . . would be women. This would be *entirely* due to the medical school enrolment and graduation patterns of 30 or more years earlier."

For groups that may have suffered past discrimination, such age structures can be valuable in understanding their present distribution in the workforce. Older people within these groups will be concentrated in lower-paying jobs, whereas their more numerous offspring will still be in school or will have entered the workforce too recently to have advanced very far. Thus the gross employment profile for this population may vary from the national average without this resulting from any present-day employer discrimination. A number of recently arrived immigrant groups display such an age profile.

The Canadian aboriginal population also manifests this pattern. Their median age is young, as is the educated segment of their population. In ten or twenty years overall aboriginal representation in the workforce will still appear discriminatory, while the picture will be quite different if they are compared with the general population age cohort by age cohort.

Geographic concentrations of particular populations also have an important impact on income and job prospects. All groups are not evenly distributed across a given territory. In the United States, a disproportionate number of blacks are concentrated in the Southern states, where overall incomes for whites and blacks are low. This skews the national income figures for blacks. In Canada the aboriginal population tends to be concentrated in rural or remote areas where employment prospects are limited, incomes are lower, and unemployment is higher than the national average for all Canadians. There is, for instance, only a 15% difference between the share of total income derived from employment between on-reserve aboriginals and non-aboriginals living near reserves, whereas the difference widens to 23% if one compares them to the population as a whole.

Some observers have also noted that aboriginal people represent a special challenge to the assumptions of employment equity. Aboriginals are engaged in a political struggle to achieve self-government and the means to preserve and protect a traditional way of life. Employment equity, on the other hand, is based on the opposite assumption that aboriginal people should have exactly the same career and other aspirations as members of the main-stream European culture, and that they should wish to participate in that culture and its conventions, including its economic behaviours. If, however, aboriginals choose the traditional way in significant numbers, as many do now and will presumably con-tinue to do, they will always necessarily be underrepresented in the conventional workforce despite the best efforts of employers and the most "enlightened" social engineering by governments.

Accidents of history, geography, demography, and group culture are certainly not the only explanations of the concentrations of members of certain groups in particular professions that do not depend on present-day discrimination. As I've already hinted, such concentrations can be the fruit of *past* discrimination.

The Jewish community knows something of this. For centuries, Christians in Europe were forbidden by the Church from lending money at interest. Jews, not subject to such restrictions, and yet prevented from occupying many other professions, became expert at the art of managing money and to this day are often highly successful in banking, finance, real estate, and other such activities because this acquired knowledge has been passed on through generations. Later, they were excluded from public administration and the military, but not from a number of the liberal professions, such as law, medicine, and the sciences, where they again became concentrated and continue to excel to this day. Ironically, past discrimination gave them a competitive edge, which they have known how to exploit effectively.

Would it be right today to see a Jewish "overrepresentation" in these activities as evidence of present discrimination on their part against non-Jews? Perhaps they should be obliged to return some of their Nobel Prizes, where they are heavily overrepresented as an ethnic group. Is the "overrepresentation" of black athletes in major-league sports discrimination against non-blacks? Is the underrepresentation of non-aboriginal artists in the field of Inuit art a reason to take native art cooperatives to task? All this is clearly absurd.

The fact is, there are all sorts of legitimate reasons — historical, cultural, demographic — why members of particular groups might be concentrated in particular industries or professions, and the people so concentrated are often themselves minorities who have acquired considerable knowledge and talent that they would be loath to waste in order to achieve some statistically correct proportional representation across all occupations.

LOOK AT THIS SAME PROBLEM from the angle of the employer. The concentration of Germans in brewing and Yorkshiremen in coal mining was surely reinforced by normal, reasonable, and non-discriminatory (in the sense of morally wrong) hiring practices. This is especially the case if one assumes that business exists to make profits and, therefore, to be more productive than its competitors.

Hiring an employee is always a gamble. Employers do not and cannot possess all the relevant information about the abilities, talents, and potential drawbacks of the applicant seated on the other side of the desk. This will be true even when they are aided by the most sophisticated testing techniques and intensive inquiries into the candidate's background. How will the person's unique combination of emotional makeup, education, personal disposition, ambition, health, family ties, instincts, and so forth all work together on the job with the different combinations of those same things brought to the workplace by the other employees, managers, and customers? In the face of this inescapable ignorance, employers make informed guesses. Perhaps they generalize on the basis of past experience with employees who present similar characteristics to those of the candidate. A popular ground for such guessing is the knowledge the candidate already has about the work to be done. Most employers want a fully productive, well-informed employee right away, preferably with no training costs and little supervisory effort required. Hence Yorkshiremen down pits and Italians in Californian vineyards. Of course some such "proxy measures" of the future productivity of potential employees are improper, and constitute discrimination that needs to be combatted. Making such judgements on the basis of skin colour or religion is clearly not acceptable. Employers must not take the view that *only* Yorkshiremen can mine coal properly, automatically turning away all others who apply.

Government has a role to play here, ranging from impartial arbitration to provision of civil remedies and the bringing of criminal charges in cases of alleged discrimination against individuals, as well as education campaigns and acting as a model employer. Government can also do more to break down the walls that separate social groups without using instruments as crude and brutal as group employment goals or quotas. For instance, research shows that hiring by and large is *local*. This means that employers tend to hire people from the area around their business, and to recruit by word of mouth. Italian workforces in Italian neighbourhoods and Greek workforces in Greek neighbourhoods are the easily predictable result. An unintended effect is to exclude people who are outside the network: people from other neighbourhoods, people without family and friends who are in the know.

Alan Borovoy, counsel of the Canadian Civil Liberties Union, recommends, in the attempt to overcome such flaws, measures like negotiated or even compulsory requirements for employers to make "every reasonable effort" to attract racial and other minorities. Business would then be made more aware of qualified applicants from such groups who might not otherwise come to their attention. Under present laws against employment discrimination, employers would be required to treat these new applicants in a non-discriminatory manner.

Such remedies are suited to what we know about the extent and severity of the disease of employment discrimination. To go beyond such measures to the sort of comprehensive social engineering that employment equity envisages should require solid corresponding evidence of comprehensive discrimination on the part of employers as a group. Crude statistical comparisons of group representation, though, do not constitute such proof. And beyond these comparisons, the evidence of systemic discrimination by employers is actually rather thin.

In the United States, two of the top five ethnic groups, arranged in order of median family incomes, are "visible minorities" — Japanese and Chinese — and the top group has been the victim of various forms of active discrimination over many years: the Jews. Black West Indians manage to achieve 94% of the national average (compared to 62% for American-born blacks) and to maintain this differential after the first-generation, that is, after the disappearance of accent, foreign training, and other factors that might distinguish the first-generation immigrant.

A look at selected ethnic groups in Canada shows five of the top ten groups by median individual income to be visible minorities, with Japanese second, and West Indians from countries other than Jamaica and Haiti fourth, ahead of Scandinavians, Italians, Poles, Germans, and so forth. In Canada, a 1991 study for the Economic Council of Canada found that on the basis of a comparison of education, occupation, sex, language, province of residence, and so on, there was "no significant discrimination against immigrants in general." This also revealed the absence of any "generalized tendency to discriminate against visible minorities."

In a separate study for the Economic Council, black and white actors were used to play job candidates for posts advertised in the Toronto area. The black candidates got job offers more often than the whites, in a marked reversal of a similar study five years earlier in which whites had been hired three times out of four. Contrary to the advocates of employment equity, who claim that discrimination is endemic and can only be defeated by intensive government direction and involvement, the Council observed that the results of their study do not "suggest that racism has vanished . . . but our results do point to a decreasing level of prejudice in Toronto as the visible-minority population grows. This reinforces the Council's broad finding that the tolerance of Canadians for visible minorities . . . is, in fact, increasing."*

AS FAR AS WOMEN ARE CONCERNED (and one of the problems with employment equity is precisely that it lumps together disparate target groups whose circumstances and opportunities are radically different) the evidence is also weak that much of the gross statistical difference between men and women is due to employer discrimination. Overall statistics show that it is not a woman's sex that determines her career prospects, but rather her marital status and level of education. The pay and advancement prospects for single men and women are virtually identical, especially when one considers other factors that cannot be blamed on employer discrimination either, such as women's career preferences, educational choices, and differing age distribution in the workforce.

The reader may consider it regrettable, but it is undeniable, as survey data show, that women who marry choose more often than men to leave the workforce for a time, are less willing than men to

* Economic Council of Canada, *New Faces in the Crowd* (Ottawa, 1991), 30–36.

work overtime or at inconvenient times, prefer the often lower-paying jobs that permit this and are much more likely than men to accept a move to advance their spouse's career (leaving their own job in the process). Just two examples illustrate such trends among women who work outside the home: women in full-time employment on average work around 10% fewer hours than men per week (one U.S. study found the figures to be 35.7 hours versus 44 hours for men, and the *Globe and Mail* reports 1992 Statscan figures of 35.2 versus 40.4 hours respectively in Canada, a gap of 12.9%). Somehow this fact rarely comes up in discussions of the "extra shift" women work in the home compared to men. On that topic, an International Labour Organization study in 1992 showed that North American men worked more hours on average than women each week even when housework was added to the totals for each. Another study found that women had been employed on average 60% of their working life, whereas men worked more or less continuously. These and other productivity-reducing behaviours may well be laid on the doorstep of unfair social mores or the way we rear our children. They are not, though, employer discrimination, nor are they all due to our "sexist" culture, for to consider it so would be to consider women, now and in the past, less competent than men to make decisions about how to live their own lives.

One of the functions of marriage, to take an obvious instance, is to allow men and women to form an economic unit, a partnership. The partnership then makes decisions, among other things, on how to maximize their economic well-being, as well as to achieve other goals, such as having a family. Take, then, the statistically undeniable fact that women tend to marry men older than themselves, add to it the simple truth that length of time in the workforce is a crucial determinant of an employee's productivity and, therefore, value, and what follows? If a choice is to be made about which partner in such a couple should drop out of the workforce or reduce the number of hours of paid employment to take on primary responsibility for the children, economic rationality dictates that it should be the one with the lesser earning power. The obvious conclusion to draw is that the fast track to economic and employment equality is for women to marry men younger than themselves, a solution with other side benefits worth pondering.

But are we as far now from equality for men and women in the workplace as the rhetoric and popular wisdom suggest? There are many reasons for treating the conventional view with skepticism. Here are just a few.

A 1982 Ontario Ministry of Labour publication, *The Female-Male Earnings Gap in Ontario: A Summary*, stated that when productivity comparisons are made within the same narrowly defined occupations within the same establishment the adjusted (male-female wage) ratio tends to be in the range of 0.9 to 0.95. In other words, the wage gap narrowed to between 5% and 10%. And this study did not correct for marital status, which alone might well have made up the small difference that remains. Much work still remains to be done in this area, but many of the studies of women's employment patterns over the past few decades suggest similar progress, especially when comparing women and men of similar education, age, profession, and marital status.

Knight-Ridder newspapers analysed the data taken from the 1990 U.S. census and revealed that women have made notable gains at the expense of men, both in their overall share of the workforce and in their numbers at executive and managerial levels, continuing trends well in evidence before the advent of affirmative action. Comparing the 1986 and 1991 Canadian censuses, in 1986 919,690 men worked in managerial, administrative, and related occupations (that is, the coveted white-collar jobs) versus 422,280 women. In 1991 the respective numbers were 1,086,150 and 653,020. The net increase for men was thus 166,460, but for women it was 230,740, or put another way, women won 58% of the net overall increase in employment in white-collar jobs over this period. As the graph also shows, the increase from 1981–86,

THE ROAD TO EQUITY

although based on slightly different job classifications, shows a similar increase in favour of women. The bulk of this increase would have been with employers not governed by employment equity requirements.

These trends, too, are probably accelerated by larger economic transformations, such as the shift from manufacturing to services, which, overall, are more accessible to women. The U.S. census reports that in 1990, for the first time in American history, there were more people doing executive, professional, or technical jobs than making or transporting goods. White-collar jobs were up by almost 40% over the decade, while blue-collar jobs declined 2%.

In Canada, although we are constantly inundated with largely anecdotal claims to the effect that there is a glass ceiling preventing the advancement of women, and that the welcome they receive in business and industry is frosty at best, the tableau that emerges from the hard figures is, again, rather different. Take, for example, a 1989 study by the Department of Education in Quebec (*Au-delà des mythes: les hauts et les bas des travailleuses non-traditionnelles*). This study was based on extensive interviews with women studying for, or occupying jobs in, traditionally male-dominated professions. Over 85% of the workers said that their reception by their male colleagues had been favourable or very favourable, and a mere 3.8% considered harassment a serious problem in the workplace. At the university level, the female students finding their reception to have been positive — and we're talking here about such programs as engineering, law, and medicine, — were 96.8% of the sample.

As for the current portrayal of sexual harassment in the workplace as a problem of massive proportions, this is not borne out either. In the 1984 study ("Incidence of Rape and Sexual Assault in an Urban Canadian Population") that provided the much misused figure that one Canadian woman in four will be sexually assaulted in her lifetime, the 551 women surveyed were asked who their sexual aggressors were. Five percent of those who had been sexually assaulted (or less than one percent of the total sample) identified coworkers or colleagues as their victimizers. And almost half of all incidents reported occurred before the women were over eighteen, which is to say, before most of them were even in the workforce at all.

But what about the problem of the so-called pink-collar ghettos? Women, for some of the reasons already examined, as well as others, are concentrated in certain areas of employment (as nurses, teachers, secretarial and support staff, for example). Pay in some of these jobs tends to be low. The obvious conclusion: society undervalues women's work.

If only reasoning from effect to cause were so simple. The misconceptions and misunderstandings necessary to reach this view of women in the labour market are so many that they cannot all be examined here. Clarity requires, however, that we touch on a few of the issues raised.

If it is the case that a concentration of men in a particular field *causes* high wages to be paid and is a sign of the value society attaches to that work, how are we to understand the low wages paid to (overwhelmingly male) taxi drivers? Or the decline and disappearance of all those (male) blacksmiths? What about the low esteem in which garbage collectors and many other manual (and mainly male) workers are held in public opinion?

While there can be no denying that men tend to dominate in a number of high-status professions, they also tend to dominate in a number of low-status professions, which are always left out of account when wage gaps and pink-collar ghettos are discussed. One study comparing the status actually attached by American public opinion to a wide range of occupations found that, overall, female-dominated ones had a slightly higher status than male-dominated ones. People think highly of teachers, nurses, and many other service occupations in direct contact with the public.

Perhaps this example gives us some insight into what is meant by how society values different jobs or occupations. The simple fact is that people's subjective evaluations of certain occupations, and of the people performing them, does not determine what those occupations pay. Several high-status occupations (such as the clergy) are exceedingly *ill paid*. The most wanton, drug-soaked rock singers (of any sex whatsoever) may make millions. The economic value of anything — jobs, cars, houses, steel, software, Big Macs — is determined by something quite different: supply and demand. There is no objective measure of the worth of things or of labour.

How quickly we have forgotten, as a culture, that we went through a long period when we believed otherwise, with economically disastrous results. Centuries were spent in the Middle Ages debating how to determine the just price for commodities, so as to have an objective measure of when sellers were taking advantage of buyers. Church authorities constantly second-guessed market prices or, in such cases as lending money at interest, outlawed the market altogether. The best minds, such as the Medieval Schoolmen, wrestled with this problem of value and were defeated by it. Their conclusion, the right conclusion, was that the factors going into making the value of a thing or a job were so vast and complex that no mere human could ever know them all.

Those who ignore history are condemned to repeat it. Pay equity, which is based on this erroneous notion of the just price for labour (in this case women's labour), is an object lesson in this vexing verity. Pay equity's apologists maintain that nothing is simpler than to determine the value of a job: compare it to other jobs. Break a job down into its component tasks, its level of responsibility, its required qualifications; compare it to what those same components seem to fetch when attached to other occupations; and presto, any difference between what a component is worth when attached to mostly female occupations, and what its worth when attached to mostly male occupations, is pay discrimination.

This sort of logic is favoured by the average home owner. The value of my house ought to be easy to determine. I'll tot up the value of the building materials and the labour that went into it, the amount I've invested in roofing, new furnaces, and so forth, factor in its location, and I've got an objective measure of its worth. Wrong. Anyone who bought when the market was high and tries to sell when the market is low, or anyone who didn't foresee the noisy convenience store that was built behind the house last year, anyone who has put a swimming pool in a house in a down-and-out neighbourhood has learned the painful truth that what has been done in the past is not what determines prices now and in the future. That doesn't mean that prices are irrational; they simply reflect the sum of beliefs on the part of all buyers and sellers about the value of things. That, in its turn, is determined by their beliefs about the relative scarcity of things. If there are lots of buyers and few sellers prices go up.

It is, however, wrong to believe that our subjective evaluations of the status of particular things or occupations in the abstract *determines* their market price. Yet this idea underpins the notion that society undervalues women's work. A moment's reflection will show that what people will pay for doesn't depend on the status they attach to the profession of the person doing or selling it. You may think lawyers are a species that could usefully and blamelessly be exterminated, but you'll pay the going rate to get one if someone sues you or you want to be certain that your children receive their intended legacy. And you'll think the lawyer charges too much, while the lawyer will be convinced that he or she is selling legal services too cheaply. Such is the self-love of human beings; we value ourselves too highly, while earnestly believing others should give us whatever we want.

Fortunately, allowing the labour market to set wages frees us from the impossible task of having to get people to agree on the value of things. The price in a freely functioning market, with lots of buyers and sellers, represents precisely the meeting point between what sellers *and* buyers believe their commodity (in this case labour) is worth.

An enduring prejudice of our economically benighted age is that somehow employers alone fix the cost of labour (at least where there is no union and no collective bargaining). Nothing could be further from the truth. Employers, as research consistently shows, are wage takers, not wage makers; they must pay the going rate. If they fail to do so, they either face a chronic shortage of workers, or they have to accept workers with low productivity. Either way, they endanger their competitive standing. The price is thus an objective fact (it does not depend on a one-sided view of the worth of its object), which is driven by a subjective reality (the sum of everyone's opinion of the worth of that object). The same cannot be said for the worth of labour determined by pay equity studies, despite all their trappings of careful scientific objectivity. If they were objective in substance, all the firms in the pay equity industry would arrive at the same conclusions about the worth of particular jobs. They do not — not by a long shot. If they were objective they would attach similar value to different elements making up those jobs, such as academic qualifications versus work experience. They do not. If they were objective, they would give as much attention to the fact that by their own measures, many male-dominated jobs are underpaid relative to other male-dominated jobs. They do not.

Like employment equity, pay equity is a wrongheaded attempt to find "justice" in the way the economy distributes things like jobs and wages. Finding nothing they recognize as a pattern of justice in the abstract, they conclude that the distribution is unjust, the result of discrimination, and that it must be corrected.

Put these appealing prejudices aside just for a moment. Suppose, for the sake of argument, that a great many women wish to have children. Suppose, too, that they want the flexibility to be able to spend as much time with them as possible in their early years. Suppose, again, that their husbands tend to be older than them and, therefore, have greater earning power. Might such women actually be quite willing to choose work requiring fewer hours in paid employment per week, demanding a lower investment in

terms of education or training, where an absence of several years
from the labour force would not too badly affect employability,
where employment is plentiful rather than highly paid, easing
moves to promote the career of the higher-earning partner, as well
as their own eventual return to the labour market? Might these be
the qualities attached to many of the jobs in the so-called pink-collar
ghettos? Might the low pay in these jobs, therefore, reflect a large
and steady supply of willing workers relative to demand? Might
the whole thing be quite sensible after all? And might employer
discrimination or society's evaluation of women's work be largely
irrelevant, where it is not a red herring?

EMPLOYMENT EQUITY AND PAY EQUITY, then, like any
government policy that obliges employers to direct their attention
to the membership of their employees in arbitrary population
groups, rather than on their productive capacity, doubly handicaps
those employers. On the one hand, their costs are increased:
inflexibility, increased payroll costs, high reporting costs, intrusive
regulation, pressure to hire less productive employees in order to
achieve statistical balance, and reduced access to individuals who
may possess the talents and characteristics that contribute to
success in a particular industry. On the other hand, many of their
international competitors are not so limited.

Perhaps, though, this is alarmist. Canadian employment equity
programs, for instance, have generally been careful to avoid the
quotas that characterize American affirmative action programs.
Canadian governments like to place the accent on working with
employers to agree on ways of increasing minority participation
in the workforce, through identifying underrepresented groups
and agreeing on positive steps such as new hiring procedures and
targets or goals for hiring particular groups, rather than using
inflexible quotas. The 1984 Royal Commission Report, *Equality*

in Employment, by Justice Rosie Abella, specifically recommended, "No quotas should be imposed."

But the American Civil Rights Act of 1964, on which most American affirmative action programs are based, was also hedged about with such disclaimers. Senator Hubert Humphrey, the act's sponsor, was emphatic that it "not require an employer to achieve any kind of racial balance in his workforce by giving preferential treatment to any individual or group." Sections were included in the act to make explicit that employers were not required to redress mere statistical imbalances through preferential treatment of individuals or groups. Under section 706(g) employer responsibility was limited to his or her own "intentional discrimination."

This clear legislative intention was slowly whittled away by Executive orders, judicial interpretations (which one Supreme Court judge found worthy of "escape artists like Houdini"), and actions by the executive agencies charged with the administration of the Act. This change was the direct result of a preoccupation with statistical results of antidiscrimination policies as measured by the composition of the workforce of particular employers. But if differences in group representation are not necessarily the result of employer discrimination, then such statistical differences can and will exist in the workforce of employers who exercise no improper discrimination whatsoever.

The persistence of the patterns, however, is taken as *evidence* of such discrimination, and its continuation under a regime of voluntary quotas and goals is taken as proof that such a regime is ineffective. Ever more heavy-handed and intrusive government involvement becomes justified and leads to quotas, in practice if not in name, as acceptable (to government) levels of employment of various groups becomes a cost of doing business if one wants to avoid constant bureaucratic interference.

Indeed, the Ontario government, in its Employment Equity Act, has dropped almost all pretension of a "voluntary" program not relying on quotas. Without a single reference to mitigating factors such as competence or merit or qualifications, the Act requires simply that "every employer's workforce, in all occupational categories and at all levels of employment, shall reflect the representation of Aboriginal people, people with disabilities, members of racial minorities and women in the community."

Advocacy groups are starting to appeal to federal and provincial human rights tribunals on the basis of the corporate employment equity reports now required by legislation in many areas. They allege that these reports show that not enough is being done by employers for employment equity target groups. The reports are advanced as proof of discriminatory behaviour. In preparation for the review of the federal act, interest groups are already lobbying hard for mandatory quotas and guidelines and an enforcement agency.

Perhaps it is all worth it in the end, though, if the result really is an increased range of career choices for groups that have not had as wide a choice as others in the past. But even this last refuge is an illusory one. Affirmative action in the United States, and now employment equity in Canada, haven't just failed to help those members of minority groups who most need it. The overall effect of both has been to harm those who are the supposed beneficiaries. Ditto for pay equity.

The experience of universities in the United States is a case in point. Since the imposition of affirmative action, the salary and promotion prospects of the best-qualified black academics have surpassed those of similarly qualified white academics, whereas the prospects of the least-qualified black academics (measured by degrees and publication record) are still behind those of similarly qualified whites. As the study that produced these figures noted, "Insofar as this is attributable to affirmative action pressures, it suggests that the program has had its greatest financial impact on those blacks who needed it least." This is not surprising. If a premium is to be placed on hiring employees from some group whose makeup has nothing to do with competence or ability, employers will aggressively recruit members of that group with established qualifications; they can be fairly certain that these individuals will perform well. Employers will thus bid up the terms available to such people, while passing over less stellar candidates. These are not, presumably, the people employment equity programs are intended to help, for this merely increases the chances for advancement of those members of minorities who are already successful in the field. The aim, however, should be to help those people on the margins of the profession, those trying to gain a foothold on the basis of weak qualifications in a field where they are largely untested. Employment equity, however, does something quite different.

In the atmosphere such programs create, potential employees will be extremely hard to get rid of if they prove to be incompetent or otherwise inappropriate. Not only is the qualified recruiting pool in which replacements might be found already limited, but the firing of minority persons can give rise to lawsuits for discriminatory treatment in which the burden of proof is on the employer to show that the dismissal was not motivated by bigotry. The dismissal becomes part of a larger pattern of treatment received by minorities (as opposed to unqualified or incompetent individuals) by the employer. When one fires a poor non-minority employee, one only takes on the employee. When one fires someone who falls within a government-defined target group, one runs the risk of taking on whole government-designed and -financed mechanisms for the enforcement of employment equity. The predictable result: minority persons with marginal qualifications have higher hurdles to jump than others with similar qualifications in an employer's eyes.

Studies bear this conclusion out. Since the inception of affirmative action in the United States, progress has not been measurably faster for the target groups. The real trend toward improvement of affirmative action's target groups' prospects began in the United States with the civil rights movement in the early 1960s. Perhaps ironically, that movement aimed precisely at removing barriers to *individual* achievement and advancement. Affirmative action has done little to speed this up.

Employment equity has damaging effects on its target groups in other ways, too. A 1987 study of the effects of preferential promotions for women (promotions on the basis of sex rather than ability) found that such women consistently rated their performance more negatively, took less credit for successful outcomes, and were less eager to persist in their leadership roles; they also viewed themselves as more deficient in leadership skills. Interestingly, when aware that they had achieved their position through preferential treatment, the female subjects of this study felt their work to be of little value even when by objective standards they were performing well.

A similar 1991 study found that when women knew that they had achieved managerial responsibility as a result of preference rather than personal merit, they tended to avoid tasks that would make them visible and increase their chances of moving further ahead. Moreover, the study's authors suggest, "because avoiding demanding tasks is likely to create a self-defeating cycle in which such women's self-confidence is perpetually undermined," this whole pattern of preferential treatment harms both women's well-being and career progress.

Shelby Steele, the black American author and social critic, sees this as being one of the hidden traps of affirmative action for blacks. In *The Content of our Character* he says that the effect of preferential treatment — the lowering of standards to increase black representation — puts blacks at war with an expanded realm of debilitating doubt, so that the doubt itself becomes an unrecognized preoccupation that undermines their ability to perform, especially in integrated situations. He goes on to note the great irony that, at a time when American universities are bending over backward — through admissions quotas, black studies programs, intercultural sensitivity training (training in the sensitivities of members of other cultures in a multicultural society), and black theme halls of residence — to make a place for blacks, blacks are dropping out of those same universities in record numbers. The number of blacks completing PhDs has actually declined since the onset of affirmative action. If this continues, affirmative action programs will be obliged to hire university professors without PhDs in order to meet their quotas, so that those hired will be even less qualified and more prone to debilitating doubt.

A key employment equity objective is to pressure employers to hire, train, and promote target group members whom they otherwise would not hire in order to break a historical pattern of discrimination. But as we've seen, if one is hired on the basis of some non-job-related criterion like sex or race or disability, invariably, incompetent people (in terms of capacities or preparation), as well as competent ones, will be hired and promoted. Leave aside the damage done to employers, students, and customers by such incompetence. Leave aside, too, the higher costs associated with getting rid of such incompetents compared with non-target group incompetents (of whom there are many). The evidence is clear that the experience of being promoted beyond one's present level of competence can lead to a great deal of stress, self-doubt, and loss of confidence, especially for members of the target groups, who may already lack self-confidence. The result in many cases may well be not equalized opportunities, but hurt people.

One particularly good example of this situation comes from the program set up by a number of Canadian universities to increase the number of aboriginal lawyers by lowering admissions criteria to law faculties for aboriginal students. In her 1977 report to the Department of Justice evaluating this program, Hope MacLean painted a sombre picture of its success. Not only were many of the people admitted to the program patently unqualified, but their future prospects were blighted by failure at an undertaking for which they were ill prepared. MacLean quotes several students who regretted having accepted the fast track and wished they had been required to meet something much more like the standard admissions requirements. Those aboriginal students who did take the usual route, on the other hand, had little difficulty in succeeding.

No evaluation of the effects of these equity programs would be complete without a glance at the perceptions of the colleagues of target group members. In the curious atmosphere created by employment equity, non-target group members who are hired or promoted in spite of the program's existence are assumed by themselves and their coworkers to have, in one writer's phrase, "instant credibility." Target group members, on the other hand, no matter how competent, are thought of as having been hired or promoted because of their group membership. Again, the effect is to call into question even the individually merited achievements of members of the target groups. Research shows that this attitude is widespread.

Whether they are right or wrong to feel this way, coworkers feel very strongly that such preferential treatment is unfair, and this can only harm the prospects of the supposed beneficiaries of employment equity. A 1991 New Zealand university study on this point concluded that preferential policies, whether based on sex or ethnic origin, were perceived as unfair. Moreover, the level of injustice was directly related to the discrepancy between the qualifications of successful and unsuccessful candidates. Interestingly, the sense of injustice *increased* when the preferential treatment resulted from a program imposed by government.

The alleged beneficiaries of employment equity policies are aware of these problems and their views of the programs in question do not vary significantly from those of the rest of the population. In the New Zealand study, women were just as likely as men to find unfair preferential policies based on sex. As Thomas Sowell pointed out in 1982, according to a Gallup poll, 64% of blacks and 80% of women reject preferential treatment in employment or college admission. Indeed, the poll could find no racial, regional, income, political, or other group in favour of this central principle of affirmative action.

Support for employment equity-type policies, though, *is* related to socioeconomic status: the well-off support them more than the poor. This may appear paradoxical until one considers that the evidence available suggests that these policies increase disparities in family income in favour of the well-off. While this may run counter to the way we imagine the world to work, it is easy to see how it might happen. Families, we should recall, are economic units as well as units of emotional support and so forth. Well-off men benefit from the greater opportunities preferential policies create for their wives and daughters (which may also explain why men in their mid-fifties with grown daughters are most likely to promote women employees). Well-qualified women, like well-qualified blacks, benefit most from affirmative action in the United States. On the other hand, women from more traditional working-class backgrounds suffer because of reduced opportunities for their men.

With our attention in this essay now focused on women, the time has come to touch on ways in which the equity addressed exclusively to them — pay equity — harms their interests, albeit in slightly different ways than employment equity.

REDUCED TO ITS ESSENCE, pay equity substitutes bureaucrats' and interest groups' opinions about the worth of labour for the worth established by the interplay of supply and demand in the market. But the pay of secretaries or bookkeepers or clerical workers is not just an abstract number that we can change at will for some other equally abstract number, leaving everything else in the economy as it was. When pay equity decrees a new wage for, say, secretaries, a complex series of effects is set in motion. The reason: people assume that the price of secretarial workers, like any other price, is a signal about supply and demand. People react to these signals, and these reactions have consequences.

Let us suppose that, following a pay equity decree, secretaries become more expensive overnight. Somehow the employer must pay for this increased cost. There are two principal ways of doing so. One is to increase the productivity of the person now being paid that wage. The other is to turn to alternative — but now relatively less expensive — sources for the same service. In either case, the employer is naturally seeking to get a return in productivity equal to the purchase price. Increased productivity might come from making the same person do more typing, filing, and telephone answering, or from expanding the person's work into new fields, such as bookkeeping or dispatching. The result is either fewer people doing secretarial work or ever higher qualification hurdles for prospective employees to jump, as they have to demonstrate higher competence levels in more fields.

Secretarial workers also illustrate rather well the notion of alternative sources of the same service. When a wage is raised, it doesn't leave the person receiving it in the same competitive position as before, certainly not in the case of secretaries. Here women are not just in competition with men for scarce jobs and wages. They are also in competition with technologies that can supplant them in many forms of work.

For example, I now much prefer to do my own typing on a word processor, to the point that when I write I actually do all my composing at the keyboard. The finished product is entirely controlled by me, and I don't have to take the time to explain laboriously in words to someone else exactly the picture I have in my mind of the finished product; nor do I have to explain, justify, or apologize for changes and corrections as they arise. As such technologies become more widespread, the whole *métier* of secretary becomes redundant and inefficient, having been completely displaced by computers and laser printers. Voice mail is only one more in a series of technologies that are potential competitors to humans. Human wages, therefore, are deeply influenced by the (ever falling) price of these alternatives. Supply and demand doesn't just take account of the supply and demand of a single commodity. It puts a dollar value on choices between alternative ways of accomplishing a particular end or goal. If I can do my own secretarial work more cheaply by investing in machinery, then I have more money left over to do other things I also want to do. These are the calculations every sensible employer — and consumer — must make.

The women who are helped by pay equity are, again, those with the most invested in themselves in terms of education, training, and work experience — those who can provide the best productivity for the money and offer something competing technologies cannot. The new entrant onto the labour market, like the ill educated worker or the one returning to work after an absence of several years, will find herself in a losing battle with her better endowed sisters. These examples can be applied to many of the traditional fields of female employment.

Since prices normally reflect supply and demand, they are useful in illustrating another way that pay equity turns into a disadvantage for women. A rising wage is a signal of a rise in demand for people to do the work relative to supply. When choosing careers, people naturally look at what they are paid, among other things. In this way, market wages signal to people where it is most profitable to invest time and money in their human capital, that is, in their education and training; the market is a signal of opportunities. By uncoupling wages from market pressures, pay equity completely distorts these signals. Jobs with limited futures, in direct competition with supplanting technologies, jobs where women have traditionally been concentrated, will be made to appear to have falsely rosy futures. And since only the very best and most productive workers will be able to land these jobs (as they will be much scarcer than their wage suggests), the people who will be attracted into these fields may well be those best equipped to succeed in a number of the less traditional fields for women. Pay equity thus works at cross-purposes to employment equity in several ways.

One final point on the perverse effects of pay equity on women. Child-care workers have been among the groups claiming and receiving pay increases under pay equity. Assuming that government does not merely pass on the extra burden of this through taxation (which has other problems that cannot be dealt with here), the employer must get the extra money out of his or her customers. That means that the price of child care goes up.

Like the plotline of many a Hollywood sequel, the consequences require no imagination to foresee, but still have some entertainment value. The value to a family of a parent (in most cases the mother) staying home to look after the children goes up accordingly, because the family would have to pay that much more to replace the previously free (in monetary terms) service. This increases the economic incentive for women to stay home, especially if they fall into the low-skill, little-work-experience category that pay equity contributes mightily to pricing out of the market.

PUTTING PAY EQUITY reluctantly to one side again, there are still some items on the bill to be presented to the beneficiaries of employment equity that we would be remiss if we did not review. Employment equity raises with a vengeance all the complexities and mysteries of individual identity. The suggestion has been made, for instance, that fear of being singled out for unwanted special treatment may help to explain the reluctance of members of a number of the target groups to identify themselves on the employer surveys needed to establish the group composition of the workforce. When Bell Canada first tried to survey its 60,000 employees, 20% refused to return the questionnaire, and management suspected that many of these individuals were target group members. As a result, managers took the second survey in hand personally, thus producing "improved" data. But improved data are no solution to the underlying problem. Many people who could qualify as "disabled" (that is, who "are limited in the kind or amount of work they can do") do not consider themselves disabled, and do not wish to be singled out for any kind of compensatory treatment. They, like most people, think they can and should be able to succeed on their merits, and want to be seen to do so by their colleagues.

The painful subjectivity of the definition of "disabled" (who is not, by this definition, disabled in one way or another?) highlights the ways in which the intricacies of our identities confound the simplistic worldview of employment equity. Nowhere is this more obvious than in the arbitrariness of the categories and of the choice of target groups in employment equity. At least in the case of women there can be relatively little dispute as to who is one and who isn't, although in these days of sex change operations even this simple verity may be open to attack.

Racial identification opens an altogether different horizon. If employees may "self-identify" and there is no control over how they do so, why not claim to be a member of a racial minority if there are benefits attached? And if there are controls, do we not become like those racist societies (such as South Africa or the American South) who were and are famous for their attention to the tiniest fraction of another race's blood coursing through someone's veins?

The worst, however, is the category of disability. One person's disability is another's advantage. Blindness might be an asset in a job requiring great aural concentration and discrimination, such as a sound or recording engineer, or a radio technician. If a person with one kind of disability develops a compensating ability, is he or she advantaged or disadvantaged by the original disability? Carlos Costa, the first swimmer with no legs to make the fifty-two-kilometre crossing of Lake Ontario, said it all. Without his disability, he observed, he might not have had the toughness to become a successful marathon swimmer.

On the other hand, many disabilities associated with the mind cannot easily be compared in their effects on different persons. A mental condition felt by one person to be debilitating and intolerable might be found by another to be simply a fact of life and in no way disabling. Someone with spatial-orientation difficulties might simply go through life vaguely amused at how often they get lost when trying to follow a map. Another person with exactly the same objective difficulties might experience them as humiliating, frightening, and threatening. Because of the subjective nature of this kind of disability, we, in fact, have no way of knowing how many disabled people there are and in what proportions they exist in the labour market.

As for the list of employment-equity target groups itself, the question comes immediately to mind, "Why these groups and not others?" There is ample empirical evidence to document the many subtle and invidious forms that discrimination takes, and it is by no means limited to these arbitrarily defined groups. These other forms of discrimination are very damaging to the members of particular groups, but receive no recognition or compensation from employment equity because it reflects a particular set of tastes or priorities, a list of the discriminations that are most offensive to the most powerful interest groups of the day.

Any such list, however, is bound to be discriminatory and arbitrary. It will always create new grievances among people who feel (in many cases justifiably) that they have been disadvantaged in some way. They will not be comforted by the fact that certain groups have gained compensation merely because they happened to be the apple of the roving eye of the most powerful political force in the land: middle-class guilt.

Some of the other forms of documented systemic discrimination against identifiable groups include widespread social and economic practices and prejudices harmful to the vertically challenged (short people), the horizontally challenged (fat people), the denominatively challenged (people whose names evoke negative images, as opposed to people on whom parents bestowed "power names"), the aesthetically challenged (the ugly), the prosodially challenged (people with odd or hard to understand accents), the sinistrally challenged (the left handed), and on and on. A derisive snort is the only retort usually given when this problem is raised, followed by the claim that these other kinds of discrimination somehow don't really count. But if employment equity as a policy is really inviting us to consider the claims of individuals who have had their interests and self-esteem damaged by insensitive or hostile social attitudes and employment practices, this response is simply wrong, a brazen bluff that should be called. By what occult art do they pretend to be able to divine, one Nobel laureate in Economics asks, "whether people have made such use of their opportunities as they ought to have made, and how much effort of will or self-denial it has cost them and how much of their achievement is due to circumstances"?

The most likely explanation for the scoffers' reaction is that they know that a generalized policy of attempting to compensate all victims of identifiable discrimination is liable to reveal that virtually everyone has suffered, in greater or lesser degree, from some form of identifiable and damaging discrimination. This being the case, one might ask, why are the interests of one arbitrarily defined group of people being damaged by employment equity (through even greater obstacles to getting a job because of quotas, for example) in order to promote the interests of another equally arbitrary group? Especially when the members of the employment equity target groups who have suffered the least from discrimination are the greatest benficiaries.

IRONICALLY, IN THIS ERA OF EQUITY by decree, the 1992 Nobel laureate in Economics, Gary Becker, first became famous for rigorously demonstrating that the incentives in a functioning employment market act to undermine discrimination.

If discrimination drives down the price a productive employee can claim in the market, that represents a profit opportunity for the entrepreneur who is willing to brave the disapproval of the majority. Such defectors, if not prevented from doing so, will tend to bid up the minority's wages to the market level.

An impressive example of this principle is the participation of black athletes in professional sports. For a number of years there was a tacit agreement among ball clubs not to hire or use black players, in spite of their talents. It only took one defector, however, to bring this whole precarious racist edifice crashing down. When the Brooklyn Dodgers brought Jackie Robinson up from their Montreal farm team to play in the National League in 1947, a floodgate was opened. The competitive pressure created by bringing in this new talent forced even the most reluctant baseball owners to fall into line. Even if they thought their fans didn't want to watch black players, they knew those same fans wanted to lose to other teams even less.

Within ten years professional baseball was fully integrated. It came so fast and the previously excluded talent was so good, that for seven consecutive years not one white man won the National League's Most Valuable Player award. One conclusion that can be drawn from this and similar examples is that the longer the exclusion lasts, and the stronger it is, the greater becomes the pressure to break it down. A pool of underused but qualified applicants grows and grows, making the cost of *not* using them mount and mount.

It is for precisely such reasons that regimes like the American South or South Africa rely on government and laws to enforce discrimination, because otherwise enough employers will prefer to make better profits than to put themselves at a competitive disadvantage. This is amply documented in the case of the American South. Under competitive market conditions (that is, no legislated discrimination and numerous employers) from the end of the Civil War to the end of the nineteenth century, black incomes rose faster than white incomes in the South. One author notes that "southern newspapers and magazines were full of recriminations among white employers because they failed to stick together in resisting the pressure of higher pay for blacks." The declines in the economic status of blacks that came later were primarily the result of government action, not the functioning of markets. Discriminatory laws and a wink and a nod in the direction of private violence gave the bigots the upper hand.

It is worth noting, in passing, that the incentive system at work in democracy is the reverse of what has just been outlined. This, too, is well illustrated by the Old South. Under markets and competition, rewards go to the minority willing to brave the fury of public opinion. No twinges of liberal conscience are needed, no unslakeable thirst for social justice; all that is necessary is the profit opportunity that is created by the very fact of discrimination.

Under democracy, in contrast, lawmakers are rewarded for pandering to the wishes of powerful interest groups that sway majority opinion, no matter how ill informed or morally reprehensible their wishes. Defectors from the majority view in public life, as Alexis de Tocqueville so trenchantly noted, generally suffer the fate of abandonment by their friends and of ignominious defeat on election day. We assume too much when we see politics as the best or even the only route to take to improve the chances and conditions of hitherto despised and neglected minorities.

THERE CAN BE NO DOUBT that "equity" programs find their genesis in a sound idea: that misleading stereotypes and unexamined practices from the past can pose unjustified and arbitrary barriers to individual advancement and proper pay policies. There is always room for improvement of the rules of recruitment, employment, and the marketplace so that individuals are treated fairly. There is also a key role for government to play in combating child poverty and improving access for everyone to those things that really *do* shape career chances: high-quality education and an efficient labour market. Finally, there is much that government can do to encourage attitudes of tolerance and social responsibility.

Government is mistaken, however, in trying to manipulate gross employment outcomes directly. Especially at a time when demographic change is increasingly obliging employers to turn to non-traditional sources of employees, this seems one area where government should stick to setting the rules of fair competition, instead of trying to fix the results. But then the real beneficiaries of the fixing are the governments that have discovered in employer-financed equity programs a cheap way of projecting an image of social activism at a time of fiscal restraint.

Racism, Property,
and Aboriginal Culture

Andrea: Unhappy the land that has no heroes! . . .
Galileo: No. Unhappy the land that is in need of heroes.

Bertolt Brecht, The Life of Galileo

A PANEL I was on in Halifax last year included a young aboriginal law student who was there to discuss the aboriginal self-government provisions of the Charlottetown Accord. A member of the audience earnestly asked her for an example of the ways in which European institutions had interfered in her people's way of life, to illustrate why aboriginal people needed self-government. She chose as an example the law of property, a subject she had been set to study in one of her classes for a seminar presentation. Her detailed study of the conception of property in Canadian law was a revelation to her, she said. Her traditional Mi'kmaq (Micmac) upbringing had imparted to her a conception of life so different, she declared, that she considered the very institution of property itself a form of racism against aboriginal peoples. They were violated in their culture and their morality by being in any way associated with it. Nor was this viewpoint limited to the Mi'kmaq; it was held as a general truth for all aboriginal peoples.

Having participated in the negotiations of the Charlottetown Accord, and in much of the public consultation that preceded it, I had often heard the claim that the law of property was singularly offensive and foreign to aboriginal peoples. I had heard, too, that it was racist because it made no place for the wholly different practice that existed in Canada before the arrival of the Europeans. But this time something was different; the reason for the public's uncritical acceptance of the demands of national aboriginal organizations, and their lionization of aboriginal leaders like Ovide Mercredi, suddenly became much clearer to me. The aboriginal people are cultural heroes to the urban middle class of this country. Canada's native people profess to want to live a life that corresponds to middle-class fantasies of living in accord with nature, away from city, factory, and office, being able to share rather than compete, enjoying a way of life in common with their fellows. The institution of property and its rejection is intimately linked to this romantic longing. Property symbolizes all that is corrupt, competitive, and controlling in our society. A cooperative society that could endure without property would have to be morally superior to ours, because in it the true needs of each person would be satisfied, while superficial desires would not be indulged. The common good would not be obstructed by stubborn individuals clinging to their narrow right to land or goods.

Perhaps no federal constitutional proposal was so widely mocked and disdained as the one that sought to place the right to property in the Charter of Rights and Freedoms. I suspect this was due to a reluctance on the part of this same middle class to bring the dirty little secret out into the open that property, shameful as it is, is an absolutely central institution to our form of life. That aspect of middle-class denial, however, is not my concern in this essay.

We will hear more and more in the coming decade on the issue of Canada's aboriginal peoples and their right to their own public institutions. The subject of property raises, therefore, three questions worthy of further reflection: (1) whether or not property as we conceive it was and is an alien concept to aboriginal peoples;

(2) whether a society without property would be morally superior; and (3) whether the institution of property can provide us with the most promising basis for aboriginal self-government, a basis that would be respectful of aboriginal sensibilities, and yet respectful, too, of Canadian traditions of individual rights and freedoms.

Property as a Concept
Alien to Aboriginal Peoples

IN MY ATTEMPT TO UNDERSTAND more deeply wherein lay the incompatibility between aboriginal culture and property, I concluded that the supposed incompatibility is largely an illusion based on a misunderstanding of the institution of property in both societies. Superficial differences in the grounding and practice of property, particularly in historical context, have been magnified out of proportion, while the underlying shared logic has been ignored or misunderstood.

The account of the aboriginal tradition's hostility to property, in thumbnail sketch, seems to run like this: aboriginal identity is based on a view of the universe in which all inhabitants are merely parts of a larger whole. This "organic" interdependency establishes a web of duties for all individuals based on an understanding of their proper relation to nature, the Great Spirit, and the community. These responsibilities entail no corresponding individual rights. The latter is a foreign concept, as members of this society find it inconceivable that they could have interests divergent from those of nature and tribe. Hence, our notions of property are incomprehensible to them because such notions centre on an idea of individual control in isolation from the guiding intelligence of the Great Spirit and in defiance of our mutual interdependence, not only between people, but between earth, sky, animals, and the human race.

One of the most eloquent and often quoted depictions of this

Brian Lee Crowley

moral order, particularly with respect to property, is found in the reply of the Squamish chief Seattle to the request that his tribe sell their land to the arriving American settlers. He said, in part, "The President in Washington sends word that he wishes to buy our land. But how can you buy or sell the sky? The land? The idea is strange to us. If we do not own the freshness of the air and the sparkle of the water, how can you buy them? . . . This we know: the earth does not belong to man, man belongs to the earth. All things are connected like the blood which unites us all. Man did not weave the web of life, he is merely a strand in it. Whatever he does to the web, he does to himself." This statement so much accords with the popular view of aboriginal culture and expresses such noble sentiments that it may seem discourteous and insolent to do anything but accept it at face value. Yet it is extraordinarily at variance with what we know of the actual practice of aboriginal society.

We must remember that Seattle was an acknowledged political and spiritual leader of his people, speaking on their behalf to a relatively new, powerful, and foreign people. The universal reflex in such a setting is to put one's best collective foot forward, to speak of one's people's aspirations, how they conceive of their place in the world, of their goodwill, and their spiritual nature. Perhaps Columbus made a similar speech on his arrival in the New World, and if he didn't, the representative of the Church, the spiritual guardian of the Europeans, certainly would have tried. In that speech the inhabitants would be assured that these strange new beings on their shores represented a brave people who believed in God, the Brotherhood of Man, and the Interdependence of all Peoples, who built shining cities and great civilizations. And he would have believed it to be a true representation of the best Europe had to offer. *Star Trek*'s Jean-Luc Picard regularly makes such speeches to alien races when the starship *Enterprise* goes exploring. But fine intentions should not be mistaken for reality.

It is an enduring prejudice of European civilization at least since the time of Jean-Jacques Rousseau in the eighteenth century that the "noble savage," as his era called aboriginal people, lived in a state of blessed innocence. In particular, it was thought — on the basis of very superficial anthropological study — that the aboriginal lived without the corruptions of character introduced by property. From this precarious starting point, Rousseau and many of the other *philosophes* concluded that most of European society's ills could be traced back to their root in the institution of property. Rousseau's moral indignation and denunciation of property knew scarcely any bounds, and they inspired two centuries' worth of revolution and socialist agitation.

> Finally, consuming ambition, the zeal for raising the relative level of his fortune, less out of real need than in order to put himself above others, inspires in all men a wicked tendency to harm one another, a secret jealousy all the more dangerous because, in order to strike its blow in greater safety, it often wears the mask of benevolence; in short, competition and rivalry on the one hand, opposition of interests on the other, and always the hidden desire to profit at the expense of someone else. All these ills are the first effect of property.*

Before the corruption introduced by Western society, Rousseau thought, people had no need for property, as all their needs were supplied by nature. Unsurprisingly, Rousseau is known as a forerunner of the Romantic revolt against reason. As an alternative to the constraints of modern civilization, and particularly the obstacle that property seems to represent to various forms of progress, this romantic vision is deeply appealing. In the state of nature, the institution of property would be understood as theft, since everything would belong to all, collectively. Let us not, however, repeat Rousseau's naive error of believing that there was no property in traditional aboriginal culture. To think this is to fly in the face of

---

* Jean-Jacques Rousseau, *Basic Political Writings,* HPC Classics Ser. (Indianapolis: Hackett, 1987), 67.

history, anthropological evidence, and the universal logic of human relations. All we need do is to examine several concepts that are well established in aboriginal culture and observe their inextricable ties to property.

Just one consequence of the absence of property would be a corresponding absence of the notion of theft, for example. The two are interdependent. Was there, then, no concept of theft in aboriginal society? It may be helpful to consider some aboriginal mythology. For example, in the Northern Plains Indian tale of the Fire Theft, Coyote, like the Prometheus of classical Greece, determines to steal fire from the Fire People and to make a gift of it to mankind. After elaborate preparations he and a group of swift animals trick the Fire People and steal their treasure, in retaliation for which all the animals except Coyote are killed. Coyote escapes and gives fire to human beings as a gift, another property-related notion to which we shall return in a moment. In West Coast Indian mythology there is a similar tale of how Raven stole Light from Heaven. Clearly both ideas of property *and* theft existed, and theft had severe penalties, as Coyote's cronies discovered at great cost.

But what about everyday aboriginal life? Can anyone seriously contend that the maker of a West Coast copper, or a birch canoe, or a buckskin jacket, would not have fought to prevent someone from taking it for their use without his or her consent? Can it seriously be suggested that their neighbours would not have come to their aid? Yet on what basis could such resistance be justified except by the notion that one *owns* what results from mixing one's labour with the fruits of nature? One owns one's labour, because one owns one's body; those are one's property. Property also extends to less tangible "services," such as those performed by shamans who treated the ill. According to the anthropologist Franz Boas, payment to the Shaman

> included canoes, chilkat blankets, sea otters, slaves, houses, and the daughters of chiefs. The goods accumulate during the course of the cure

as inducement payments to the spirits; but in the end, of course, they would be carried away by the shaman.*

Perhaps there is still doubt that the fundamental property on which this argument is based — property in one's person — existed in aboriginal culture. Consider, then, two ideas relative to the security of the person that are intimately linked to property: kidnapping and slavery, concepts that were well understood in aboriginal culture. Kidnapping, of course, is nothing less than taking possession of a body without the consent of the owner who inhabits it. Again mythology offers us ample proof of aboriginal awareness of the idea of kidnapping and its moral impropriety, as in the tale of Grass Woman's abduction and rescue.

As for slavery, the quotation from Boas already provides us proof of the existence of the institution, and it is amply documented elsewhere. Slavery, considered from the point of view of property, is nothing but a transfer of the ownership of the body and labour of a person from that person to another. Without a conception of property, the very idea of slavery would be incomprehensible, for the slaves would not remain under the control of their owners except by constant coercion, which would render them virtually useless. Only if slaves and owners believe in the essential right of possession and the corresponding loss of autonomy can slavery survive.

Consider something else that is closely allied to property: gifts and friendship. It is hard to conceive of friendship without gifts, which are tokens of respect and affection. Gifts can also be symbolic of the status and importance of the giver. Certainly gift giving existed in aboriginal culture. It goes without saying, however, that one cannot give what one does not own.

---

* Franz Boaz, *Kwakiutl Culture as Reflected in Mythology*, vol. 27, quoted in Joseph Campbell's *Historical Atlas of World Mythology*, vol. I (New York: Harper & Row, 1988), 191.

The famous West Coast Indian potlatch ceremony is the most obvious example of such gift giving. The very name comes from the Chinook word *patshatl,* meaning gift, or giving, and according to one authority, the "institution of the potlatch was of a lavish, extremely formal, gift-giving ceremonial offered by a wealthy host to a large invited company, usually for the purpose of gaining or confirming social rank, prestige or privileges for himself or . . . of passing on the like to his inheritors." * Not only does the institution of the potlatch confirm the existence of private property in goods necessary to the ceremony, but the description also refers to "wealthy hosts," an idea inseparable from the concept of property.

Finally, it is helpful to dwell briefly on the concept of *sharing.* Much of the romanticism surrounding aboriginal culture comes from the notion that all was shared, that needs were satisfied for all, that the burden of shortages was equally borne by all. While not denying that sharing on this scale existed, it would be a mistake to believe that sharing resulted from an absence of property. Sharing does not imply that everyone got whatever they wanted whenever they wanted it. Each was *entitled* to certain things under certain conditions. And sharing did not extend to non-tribe members (except under extraordinary circumstances), or to those who were exiled from the tribe. Again, one cannot share with others what one does not own, and one cannot prevent others from taking what is rightfully theirs. What must interest us, then, are the *conditions of sharing,* for they, and not the superficial question of property, truly distinguish aboriginal from non-aboriginal practice. This is a matter to which we shall return shortly.

Perhaps, however, the discussion so far does not get to the heart of what is meant by the notion that aboriginal people did not share our conception of property. Particular opprobrium seems to be reserved for the idea of property in land, the notion that the earth, which belongs to all creatures and divinities, could be parcelled out

---

* Joseph Campbell, *The Historical Atlas of World Mythology,* vol. I, 251.

and access denied to all but its "owners." Again, Rousseau was a precursor of our common view, holding that

> the first person who, having enclosed a plot of land, took it into his head to say this is mine and found people simple enough to believe him, was the first founder of civil society. What crimes, wars, and murders, what miseries and horrors would the human race have been spared, had someone pulled up the stakes or filled in the ditch and cried out to his fellow man: "Do not listen to this impostor. You are lost if you forget that the fruits of the earth belong to all and the earth to no one!"*

Even worse, the commonly conceived aboriginal perspective is that property owners could use the land without due regard to the web of ecological and moral ties that bind together man, animal, and land across all geographic boundaries. It was this matter of owning land, in particular, that Seattle was referring to in the passage quoted earlier.

But again, it should not be suggested that there was no aboriginal concept of property in land. Take for instance the notion of nations, whether Western or aboriginal. Each nation has a territory, and its nationhood is defined in part by its ability to control that territory. Such control would include preventing access to outsiders or, where access is allowed, ensuring that outsiders conform to national norms of behaviour. Control of national territory also includes defence from external attacks. In short, the nation exercises a right of property over its territory, and those who are not welcome or who refuse to observe the rules are trespassers who may be killed or chased off the property. This property right was exercised with considerable vigour by the First Nations, who were known to go to war with one another over various forms of territorial incursion long before the arrival of the Europeans. A whole social class — warriors — existed precisely

---

* Rousseau, *The Basic Political Writings*, 60.

for the purpose of protecting the territorial integrity of aboriginal societies and the physical integrity of tribe members from external attack or violation. And, of course, what basis could there be for the settlement of aboriginal land claims today if both sides did not recognize the legitimacy of aboriginal title to their traditional lands?

It is true that the protection of territory does not add up to a full-blown notion of individual property in land, but acknowledging that aboriginal societies protected their land is a further step in rejecting the notion that all people were free to wander as they pleased, helping themselves to the fruits of nature wherever they were to be found. Furthermore, within tribal territories the arrangements governing land use were complex and depended on notions very much akin to our concept of property. After all, one could not knock down a neighbour's lodging because one wanted the site for one's own home, any more than tribe members could practise their horsemanship in the maize patches cultivated by tribes like the Algonquin and the Iroquois. Somehow the impression seems to have grown that this differentiation of land use and complex social cooperation was based on the simple goodwill and helpful nature of the aboriginals, and not on a regime of property rights. All land simply *was;* it was not and could not be *possessed* by anyone.

As the territorial defence example shows, however, matters were considerably more complex than that. In fact, there was a regime of *communal* property, ownership of all land being vested in the community as a whole. Tribal authorities were called upon to mediate disputes regarding the appropriate uses to which tribal resources, including land, should be put. Obligations, backed by sanctions, bound each member of the community to respect the established rights of use. This is far from being radically dissimilar to our own system. Property need not imply exclusivity; in fact, as both communes and shopping malls attest, collective control and public access are both entirely compatible with the notion of property.

The confusion that arises grows out of the same mistake that has often been made with respect to communism, a system in which, it is often believed, property has been abolished. Nothing could be further from the truth; property exists under communism, it's just that there is a unique property *holder* or *owner*. As anyone trying to build a house on a site reserved for a factory by the state in the few remaining communist countries quickly discovers, property (in the sense of an authoritative allocation of ability to use scarce resources) is very much present. The same was true in aboriginal society. Certainly alternative land uses were forbidden by those entitled to determine how tribal resources would be used, or rather, the notion of proposing non-traditional land uses simply didn't arise. There simply wasn't enough population pressure to cause land to become *scarce,* so the problem of how to decide between competing alternative uses for, as an example, tribal burial grounds, simply would not have been posed.

THE SIMPLICITY OF ABORIGINAL LIFE before the arrival of Europeans is not, in fact, indicative of a fundamental or irreconcilable cultural difference, no more than it is attributable to any absence of property. That simplicity grew out of a different order of social complexity and population density. Aboriginals lived in a face-to-face traditional society founded on a concrete shared end (for example, successful prosecution of the hunt); Europe was already groping towards the vast extended order of social cooperation we all enjoy today without having to agree on a common purpose to pursue as a society.

The traditional, organic nature of aboriginal society is graphically illustrated in the Ojibway legend of Mondawmin, the tribe member who won the boon of maize from the gods. On presenting this divine gift to the tribe, Mondawmin says, "We need no longer rely on hunting alone; for as long as this gift is cherished and taken care of, the ground itself will give us a living." In other words, where before maize there had been only one focus of all social activity, the hunt, there was now a second. All of tribal life was organized around these two activities with a division of labour (cooking, making clothing, preserving meat, gathering roots, berries, and other dietary supplements, hunting, planning defence, spiritual well-being) among tribal members. Playing one's assigned role within this overarching social organization constituted the "conditions of sharing" referred to earlier, the conditions on which the cooperative nature of aboriginal society was founded.

All such societies believe that the rules governing this cooperation, their "laws," are not made by human beings, but are the gift of the Great Spirit or some other supernatural source. Chiefs, headmen, and shamans do not make laws; they are merely mouthpieces of the deities, as Moses was of God, and as Muhammad was of Allah. Moreover, the deity gives to the community a right to exploit the fruits of nature in accordance with appropriate standards of morality, prudence, and good husbandry. Certainly this was the message of Genesis, in which Man was given trusteeship (not ownership) over the earth and, in the beginning, was forbidden to kill animals even for food. In return, the deity promises the bounty of nature, as in First Timothy, where it is said that God "richly provides us with everything for our enjoyment."

In their origins, then, traditional European societies were not so very different from aboriginal ones. Each person had a place, a role, in the social order, which was his or hers to play out, in accordance with a divine scheme. Property in land, it is true, was held by individuals, but they did so on certain conditions and incurred certain obligations towards the community.

Then what transformed Western society and made it so different culturally from traditional aboriginal societies? Simply this: under the pressures of urbanization and the growth of both technological diversity and the concept of individuality, acceptance of a shared, concrete social project began to break down. We could no longer achieve social solidarity and mutual cooperation merely from everyone's belief that their very material survival and spiritual salvation depended on their playing a predetermined role or function. Nor could cooperation continue to be based on a shared belief in a divinely directed unfolding of human affairs. The Reformation, among other things, saw to that.

The evaporation of a common belief in the good life, a common image of salvation or of communion with God, had consequences. So, too, did the growth of large cities based on commerce and a hugely diversified division of labour not organized around an unquestioned assumption about the concrete purpose or end of the work itself. The principal consequence, from the point of view of this discussion, was that people had to be able to live cheek by jowl with one another, and to cooperate, without appealing to a common standard of traditional authority and without a common project whose imperatives automatically overrode incompatible individual desires. Before, conflicts between members of the community could be resolved by authorities charged with the moral and material well-being of all. Now this basis of authority ceased to exist. The only practical alternative was very unspiritual and utilitarian. Instead of having to agree on fundamental values before being able to work together, it gradually became clear that within a single society, people could cooperate through voluntary exchange of goods and services. This is precisely the principle on which trade between communities and nations had always been carried out. As Adam Smith put it, it is not the altruism of the butcher that gets me my supper, but his self-interest.

While it may be true, therefore, that a society needs *some* common vision in order to survive and flourish, Western society radically transformed the traditional vision. Gone was an accepted concrete project around which all human activity and values were organized. In its place was substituted an *abstract* common good, one that referred to no particular set of objectives, no particular form of life. This abstract good was to allow each of us to decide for ourselves our own life plans, our own values, our own goals, whatever they might be, to develop our own personality by our own vision.

In a society with a complex division of labour, however, where university professors are dependent on publishers and computer manufacturers, where labourers are dependent on clothing and tool makers, where mothers are dependent on day-care workers and baby-food companies, we still need to know that cooperation is possible with those who do not share our vision of the good life. Traditional societies do not need this reassurance because the basic end of society is fixed, and the wealth of the group is distributed according to the contribution of each to that end.

In the absence of a concrete project, the central feature of a liberal society becomes an impersonal set of rules. Such rules guarantee freedom of choice and conscience, the "space" necessary to build a life. They also, however, establish the conditions of choice, by setting out what choices we may *not* make (for example, we cannot rob, cheat, or murder others) in the attempt to build the good life as we understand it. This abstract good of liberal society is not about the *content* of the choices that free individuals make, but about maximizing the conditions and possibilities of the choices we will then be free to use in unpredictable and surprising ways, to create ways of life hitherto unimagined. This does not imply that with modernity Western society renounced the notion that there might indeed be one right way for people to live, one fully human or best way of life. But centuries of wars between Christians, to take just one example, convinced us that even if there is such a thing as the common good or the natural harmony of human beings and the environment, reasonable people of good faith can disagree on what constitutes these things, and disputes must arise that cannot be resolved by referring to any obvious or universally agreed-upon authoritative source. Christians share a common Bible, for example, but not a common understanding of how to interpret it, nor how to live according to its precepts.

To avoid settling disputes by violence, competition over scarce resources such as land and goods would have to be settled impersonally, by market mechanisms such as price that are indifferent to the uses different people want to make of their property, and therefore do not favour one way of life over another. Property in land, originally necessary to prevent disputes among members of a settled agricultural society in the face of population growth, and to make possible the long-term capital investment necessary to make the land productive, began to offer other virtues. Property allowed people a clear idea of the area over which they could exercise control and in which others could not interfere. Within a single society, farms and monasteries, synagogues and factories, universities and markets could coexist, even though those who ran these different institutions agreed about almost nothing. Changes in use of property from one to the other could be accomplished by negotiation.

The bases of individualism flourished, but people were not obliged to be individualists. Those who wished to band together in communal enterprises, when they shared a common vision of life, also benefited from a regime of property because they did not need anyone's permission to live as they pleased. The autonomy conferred on them by property, in land, in goods, in their bodies, guaranteed them the room to conduct experiments in living, preventing them from being coerced and from coercing others. Property, which seemed at first blush a purely utilitarian development, soon betrayed a very moral character.

Moral Superiority of a Society Without Property

VIEWED FROM THIS ANGLE, aboriginal culture at the time of European contact was not fundamentally at odds with Western culture, nor incompatible with it; it was simply at a different stage of development. Aboriginals lacked the density of population in the cities of Europe; they found nature sufficiently bountiful to supply many of their needs without major capital investment; and they still enjoyed the shared concrete way of life. The conditions that gave birth to the utilitarian and moral reasons for the dispersal of property (and hence power) among many hands did not apply. Property could be vested in the community because people identified their individual good with that of the community and, therefore, were content to see resources distributed in accordance with the priorities of the community. Conflicts did not turn on the purpose or objective of the community, nor its individual members, but on the best means to achieve the given purposes.

Today many assume that Western society, and the institution of property in particular, is inherently hostile to this morally commendable communitarianism. But the exact opposite is true. Western society, by and large distributing its resources impersonally via the market mechanism, is the only practically functioning society that does not require conformity to some ideal of life from its members in order to be able to get a share of those resources. In many more "communitarian" societies, adherence and contribution to the overriding social goals give access to the community's "property": food, shelter, and so on. Let us not forget that, in certain aboriginal nations, the old who were no longer able to make a contribution to the aims of society were expected to go off alone to die. The understanding on both sides was that as soon as one ceased to be able to play one's role in the social order, one's claim on the community's property came to an end. Sharing had its price. Western society and its institutions (the institution of property, in particular) allow many different life and community projects to coexist, so long as they do so peacefully. Communities based on communalism, sharing, and unity with nature, such as Findhorn in Scotland or the Hutterites in Canada, are welcome, as long as they do not require others to pay for their way of life, and as long as all the participants are there voluntarily.

Western liberal democratic society's accent on the voluntary

nature of community membership is the real obstacle to an auto-
matic assumption of compatibility with traditional aboriginal
ways of life and, therefore, aboriginal self-government. The problem arises in this way: the self-governing society envisaged is a
"participatory community" and its moral justification lies in its
shared bonds, its self-awareness of sharing a common life, and so
on. This, however, is a description of a *subjective identity*, which
is to say that the community is morally grounded, and consensual
rule is justified to the extent that its members, taken individually,
continue to *feel part of it*.

By and large, Western society can have no objection to a
community so organized within its boundaries. Within certain very
basic limits, as long as a community's members feel a part of it and
feel that its demands are reasonable, then no moral problem arises
and the intervention of the state to protect individual autonomy
and integrity is not required or justified. What cannot be accepted
is to subject people to the demands of such a community merely
because they happen to have some common characteristic like race,
language, or class. We can assume nothing about how real flesh-
and-blood individuals feel, or what they believe in, or the sort of
life they want to live simply because they are aboriginal. To think
otherwise is to ignore the significance of five hundred years of
contact between aboriginals and non-aboriginals.

Before the arrival of the Europeans, there was almost no intellectual "space" in the aboriginal culture to imagine forms of life
outside those of the community, let alone in opposition to them.
Not only were the means of subsistence distributed by the community in accordance with its priorities, but as a traditional society,
roles were distributed to individuals based not on their personal
preferences, but on the needs of the tribe and their assessment of
individual capacity. What contact with other cultures did was to
introduce *choices* that had been inconceivable before. Over the
years, ways of living became available to individual aboriginals
that simply would not have existed in the traditional order, things

like intensive agriculture, professions, trades. Other institutions, like money and formal education, made possible further choices, as did the existence of large cities and easy means of transport.

More important than any of these, however, was the fact that a market economy and other free institutions opened up for individual aboriginal persons the possibility to act on these different choices without needing the consent of the community. It was no longer necessary to convince the tribe that the choices one wanted to make contributed to the tribe's way of life; it was no longer necessary to have the tribe's support in order to be able to earn the wherewithal to live. The existence of such choices, it must be emphasized, is inseparable from the existence of the institution of property, and the dispersion of such property into many hands. The freedom promised by the diversity of modern Western institutions remains purely theoretical if one needs the permission of the bureaucrat or the approval of the tribal elder before those institutions can be used. If such permission is forthcoming only when the choices proposed conform to some collectively defined way of life, then there are no real choices at all.

In short, the arrival of Europeans meant that the aboriginal way of life was in competition with other ways of life for the loyalty and support of its people. The institutions that Europeans brought with them did not introduce property, but made its dispersion in many hands possible, and with it the increase of choices.

TWO THINGS ARE WORTH NOTING about this state of affairs. First, some form of property as an institution is absolutely essential to the continued survival of aboriginal culture given the existence of other cultures on this continent — cultures that are in competition with aboriginal cultures for the adherence of their members. Second, the moral defensibility of aboriginal self-government depends on its remaining compatible with the basic presuppositions of Western liberal democracy. An examination of why these two statements are true leads us, by an admittedly circuitous route, back to our point of departure: the compatibility of the Western institution of property and the aboriginal way of life.

To understand the need for property as a foundation for the survival of aboriginal culture, let us revisit the argument so far, looking this time not at the relationship between aboriginal individuals and their government, but between aboriginal peoples and the rest of Canadian society. The problem aboriginals face here is that they wish to maintain their own way of life without the intervention of the Canadian government. The logic is not hard to follow: Canadians on the whole do not live according to the values and aims of traditional aboriginal ways. If aboriginals must depend on the goodwill of people who are indifferent to their objectives, their way of life will always remain precarious. Aboriginals, then, must establish a protected sphere for themselves within which they can control their own resources and make their own choices free from insensitive and paternalistic interference. What they want, in other words, is their own property.

Understandably, what aboriginal people collectively are seeking is to escape the heavy hand of control exercised over them, their land, and their resources by Ottawa bureaucrats. They want back the full rights of control and choice for their communities. They want what all other property owners in society take for granted: the rights of ownership. Again, the fact that this ownership may be collective rather than individual is neither here nor there; many kinds of property, including joint-stock companies, cooperatives, communes, and various sorts of religious and other communities of belief are held by groups of individuals. The right of control over their property can, by and large, only be exercised collectively.

This notion that the claim to aboriginal self-government is, in fact, a claim to a particularly robust kind of property right (one that excludes much Canadian lawmaking authority over aboriginal persons and property) leads directly to the second point I want to raise here: the moral defensibility of aboriginal self-government depends on its remaining compatible with the basic presuppositions of Western liberal democracy. Too often those in favour of aboriginal self-government engage in a bit of sharp logical practice in their account of the authority needed by such governments. Sometimes the position is close to the one I've just outlined, in that it maintains that there is a uniform political and cosmological view that aboriginal peoples believe in and that the problem, then, is how to protect this beleaguered minority from insensitive interference from the non-native majority. According to the logic developed so far, this is a strong argument for increased autonomy, and particularly aboriginal control over their property. (It is, however, not obvious that this argument establishes a right for aboriginals as a racial group to an order of government in competition with federal and provincial governments.)

These aboriginal values, however, are not universally shared *within* the aboriginal community, for the powers that aboriginal leaders seek could be used to coerce their own members. How else are we to understand the stiff resistance of aboriginal constitutional negotiators to the application of the Charter of Rights and Freedoms, the jurisdiction of ordinary courts over aboriginal governments, and the formal recognition of democratic participation by all members of the community in choosing leaders and in decision making? The stock reply is that such Western liberal notions are foreign to traditional aboriginal forms of government, and any attempt to impose them would be racially inspired interference and cultural insensitivity. This may be a rhetorically expedient argument for the negotiators of aboriginal self-government, but it does not stand up, for the shift in emphasis from protecting aboriginal culture from the rest of Canadian society to protecting it from dissenting aboriginals is extremely damaging to the cause of aboriginal self-government. We are now talking not about aboriginals willing themselves to be different from the rest of Canadians, but the right of some aboriginal governmental authority, whether majorities or tribal elders or some other inner cadre, to impose its views on a recalcitrant aboriginal minority. These problems are fundamentally different, but are constantly mixed up in the rhetoric of the proponents of self-government, thus obscuring the real import of aboriginal groups' claims.

In cases of disagreement within the aboriginal community itself about the right way to go about being aboriginal and maintaining the aboriginal way of life, perhaps dissenting individuals must be subject to the will of the group, regardless of individual autonomy. If so, there can be little common ground between Western liberal individualism and aboriginal self-government. And if what is envisaged is not precisely this case, where individual identity conflicts with the duty demanded by the majority (or the consensus, or the elders, and so on), then why the resistance to individual rights? Such rights, after all, will only be invoked when individuals feel that their autonomy is under threat, and not when they subjectively agree that the group's decisions embody the common good or the harmony of nature.

Disquieting consequences flow from accepting that aboriginal collective rights override those of individual aboriginals, as David Thomas, a member of the Salish Coast nation in British Columbia, can attest. At the request of his family, tribal elders ordered that Thomas be taken against his will by other band members, confined in a longhouse, and forced to undergo the initiation ceremonies of a spirit dancer of the longhouse, a traditional rite with spiritual and physical healing properties. These ceremonies involved being lifted horizontally eight times a day by men who dug their fingers into his stomach and bit his sides, being stripped naked and forced to submerge himself in a creek, and being beaten with cedar branches. Over the four-day period of the ritual he was given one cup of water each day and no food.

Because property is held collectively in the traditional aboriginal culture, including property in the person of each individual David Thomas could not assume that he had the right to do as he pleased.

Brian Lee Crowley

In the court case that followed these incidents, Thomas, who has lived off-reserve for most of his life, said that "he did not agree to undergo the treatment he received, did not authorize anyone to have him initiated as a spirit dancer and was not interested in learning about his people's culture." According to their lawyers, native leaders in British Columbia reacted with anger to the court's ruling that Thomas had been a victim of assault, battery, and wrongful or false imprisonment. Indoctrinated in a Western tradition of individual rights, Canadian judges have trouble, according to lawyer Vina Starr, in "putting collective aboriginal rights in their proper perspective." She argued, in effect, that Thomas's right to physical integrity was subordinate to the collective rights of the aboriginal nation.*

While it may be true that before the arrival of non-aboriginal cultures it would be almost inconceivable for a band member to refuse the honour of being subjected to the ritual Thomas faced, we cannot rest with such an assumption today. Thomas, like everyone, has the capacity to make choices about who he is and how he wants to live; the fact that he is aboriginal does not dictate those choices.

Those vying for complete freedom from "outside interference" through aboriginal self-government, then, run headlong into the clash of majority-minority relations in a community supposedly based on a strong subjective identity shared by all its members. Rousseau attempted to solve this moral and political problem, without success. None of his successors have done any better. Having failed to solve this problem themselves, the proponents of aboriginal self-government simply wish it away and carry on regardless, only to run squarely into the problem posed by Hobbes: Even if there is such a thing as the common good or the natural harmony of man and environment, or *the* aboriginal way of life,

* Citations for David Thomas case from "Native Rite Ruled Subject to Law," *Globe and Mail*, 8 February 1993, A6.

94

reasonable people of good faith can disagree on what constitutes these things; therefore, disputes must arise that cannot be resolved by referring to any obvious or universally agreed-upon authoritative source. In this case, what is the moral justification for coercing recalcitrants or dissidents or for excluding them from the community, as the Charlottetown Accord would have given aboriginal governments the power to do?

This, then, is one side of the argument: liberal institutions are *fully* compatible with self-government, on certain conditions. The most fundamental of these is that aboriginal communities must allow a protected sphere for individuals to grow and develop free from improper interference from the aboriginal majority or other governing authority. This is the necessary counterpart to the protected sphere for that community to develop free from improper interference from the non-aboriginal majority.

It is undeniable that the continued survival of aboriginal culture is a good in itself, and many sacrifices are no doubt justified to make this possible. We are all prone, however, to trying to pass on to others the costs of things we want for ourselves. This is what denying or undermining individual choices and autonomy does in the case of aboriginal self-government. It passes many of the burdens of preserving a traditional aboriginal way of life from those who shoulder them willingly to those who are forced to bear the load.

ARE THESE IDEAS RACIST? Are they indicative of cultural imperialism? Clearly not. On the contrary, as I have already suggested, they provide the only possible foundation for the survival of aboriginal communities.

It is only superficially paradoxical to say that Western concepts of individualism and democracy are essential to the survival of the aboriginal way of life and are not an unwarranted interference by one culture with another. The paradox dissolves when one considers that the true challenge faced by aboriginal communities in trying to survive as distinct cultural entities comes from within and not from without. Non-aboriginal culture in North America does not threaten to force itself on aboriginal peoples against their will. Quite the contrary; the threat is that individual aboriginals, faced with a choice between cultures, may well choose the non-aboriginal road if the cost (in terms of personal development, growth, economic prospects for oneself and one's children, and so forth) of remaining aboriginal is seen as too high.

It may well be the case that some of these costs are externally imposed due to paternalistic interference, failure to settle land claims, and the like. To the extent that this is so, self-government and the settlement of land claims will perhaps make traditional aboriginal ways of life more attractive to some who have been tempted to leave them behind. These will be minor and Pyrrhic victories, however, if they are regarded as providing the means to keep out the corrupting or distracting influence of non-aboriginal culture. We cannot overlook or wish away the cruel but inescapable fact that aboriginal culture is no longer alone on this continent. That being the case, aboriginal culture is always on trial in the eyes of its adherents, because they know that other possibilities exist. This single fact, the awareness of other possibilities, makes it impossible and unthinkable to isolate and protect aboriginal culture from the larger context, and makes any attempts to bolster its support through coercive means ultimately self-defeating.

Aboriginal political leaders may well be right to hold that the aboriginal tradition of decision making was consensual, and that the needs and wants of all were given their due regard before the arrival of the Europeans. The problem is that that tradition existed in the sort of social order I described earlier, in which the resources of the tribe or nation were centrally controlled and distributed in accordance with a universally accepted scheme of values and priorities. There were no realistic choices, no more than there were for the members of European societies for many centuries. The emergence of choice locates the battle for the cultural hearts and minds within the nation itself, because aboriginal culture is no longer merely an inescapable fact of life, a mental framework beyond which the imagination falters. Instead it is one choice among several, and a choice that will be judged by individual aboriginals on its own merits: on how it enriches their lives and helps them to be more fully themselves. A culture that does not allow such people to embrace new ideas and practices condemns itself to marginality and sterility — the fate awaiting aboriginal communities that adopt a defensive attitude vis-à-vis the choices their own people may make.

At the end of the day, one cannot preserve in its pristine purity a traditional way of life in non-traditional circumstances. This will be doubly true where that traditional way of life appears to limit choices beyond what its adherents find reasonable. Aboriginals are not aboriginals because they hanker after the traditional practices. What makes them aboriginal is a desire to be what they *believe that to mean,* and a desire to explore the meaning and consequences of that identity with others who share it. That is one of the principal reasons for the resistance of some aboriginal women's organizations to the Charlottetown Accord. They believed that the choices that non-aboriginal society offers to women are something that aboriginal society needs to learn and absorb. Those choices may be incompatible with traditional practices. Perhaps the practices, and not the women, must adapt.

The real challenge facing aboriginal communities is not to become stuck in a folkloric celebration of a past glory, but to explore an understanding of the past and apply its lessons to the present, to make the past live by making it come to terms with today. Arriving at this dialogue between ancient tradition and present need requires three things: first, that aboriginal governments respect the ability to choose on the part of their members. Not just in the sense of letting them vote with their feet if they disagree with the community's decisions, but in a much deeper way. Aboriginal communities must understand that they must compete with other ways of life and, therefore, must struggle to integrate the aspects of other cultures that their own people find of value. Recognition of the autonomy and rights of individual aboriginals might be a Western way of describing this, but the concept is universally applicable.

Second, this dialogue requires something recognizably like Western democratic institutions, so that every person's opinions are given public space and equal respect and weight in the choice of community leadership and policy. Traditional ways of life, then, will be upheld, because those expected to adhere to them believe in them.

Finally, this dialogue across generations requires a decentralization of power in the form of widely distributed property in the aboriginal community and its resources. Without this there will be no end to paternalistic interference in the choices that aboriginal individuals make for themselves about how they want to live.

Indian and Northern Affairs bureaucrats may now decide on almost everything to do with life on reserves: who lives where, in what standard of accommodation; what grants and subsidies will be paid to whom for starting a business or going to university. It will be of little benefit to aboriginal peoples to see the control over their lives currently enjoyed by Ottawa bureaucrats transferred to aboriginal bureaucrats. They need to make their own decisions about their own lives, and not be dictated to by paternalists of any skin colour or racial origin. There is only one way that aboriginals themselves can use their resources to build lives that correspond to their own priorities: by extending to individual aboriginals the right to a protected sphere, like the one the communities are claiming for themselves.

HOW IS THIS TO BE DONE in practical terms? I will not discuss here in detail the relative merits of this or that detailed scheme for aboriginal self-government, because most of the current ones are flawed by a basic assumption. All assume that the twin starting points for thinking about self-government are the radical incompatibility of the Western and aboriginal ways of life and the collective nature of aboriginal communities, or the belief that it is improper to inquire where the interests of individual aboriginals might lie. The interests of individual aboriginals supposedly are just whatever aboriginal leaders say they are.

The arguments I have been proposing point in the opposite direction. Aboriginal and Western societies started from similar assumptions, and the arrival of Europeans in North America only accelerated the coming, for aboriginals, of a confrontation with the joys and pains of personal choices of the most momentous kind. This further closes the gap between the dilemmas that aboriginals and non-aboriginals face in life, and in the institutions needed to support and help us in making those choices. I feel drawn inexorably to conclude that our first priority must be to recognize that the humanity linking aboriginals and non-aboriginals is more fundamental than the (rhetorically much exaggerated) cultural differences that divide us. Further, I am drawn to conclude that aboriginal institutions aiming to preserve through coercion ancient practices whose *raison d'être* has disappeared, and which fly in the face of the choices of individual aboriginals, are both morally bankrupt and doomed to failure.

The story of Western liberal democracy has been the slow, imperfect emergence of a set of institutions aimed at protecting our common humanity. Each of us can aim at a way of life that seems good, and no one may arbitrarily prevent us from pursuing such choices. The ability to choose and build an identity *is* our common humanity. Canadians seek nothing less than this for people in other countries when we defend the notion of basic human rights: the right to be free from government coercion and private violence, the right to choose one's work, to practise one's religion, to speak one's language. What if, rather than abandoning this commitment to cherishing individuality in the name of the "collective rights" of aboriginal nations, we were to try to use it as the cornerstone of new aboriginal-centred institutions? What might emerge?

Here is one stab at imagining such a possibility. This is the roughest of sketches and assumes that the details need to be worked out in individual contexts, as no account is taken here of "political realities" or existing institutional obstacles. My aim is to explore the ideas developed so far to see how they might illuminate our efforts at self-government. My hope is that by annexing new territory to the thinkable, we gain the resources necessary to breach the walls of the tiny enclave of the doable.

It would be helpful to state again the set of assumptions I bring to these issues, and on which aboriginal self-government might be based. First, no one knows the interests of individual aboriginals better than those individuals themselves. Second, what individual aboriginals believe to be an aboriginal way of life simply *is* that way of life; there is no standard outside their preferences that can be used to impose an "authentically" aboriginal way of life on them, whether it is defined by romantic fantasies of non-aboriginal Canadians, or by rent-seeking aboriginal leaders. Third, in Western European tradition, both legal and moral, there can be no warrant for regarding aboriginal culture as inherently more noble, more desirable, or more worthy of special protection than any other.

My fourth, and perhaps most controversial, assumption is that, for a variety of historical reasons, aboriginals occupy an anomalous place in Canadian society that needs to be regularized. Our common humanity and intense degree of cultural, historical, racial, geographic, and economic intermixing all deny the feasibility of separatism, as do our common citizenship and the need for our society to continue massive transfers of resources to aboriginals whatever their form of government or the size of their land-claim settlements. These realities also deny the claim that separateness justifies our abandonment of the principles of liberal democracy, of trying to imagine a set of institutions that would allow each of us to pursue our life choices within a framework of common rules. In order to be fair to both aboriginals and non-aboriginals, all people must be brought fully under the law, ending the offensive system of basing legal status and entitlements on racial origins. This means that negotiated settlements with aboriginal peoples must contain a "buying out" of any residual claims to sovereignty or other exemptions from the law.*

My final assumption is that gross injustices were committed by Europeans against aboriginal peoples in the settlement of the continent. These need to be rectified, and all land and other claims extinguished, by compensation to the descendants of those harmed. This is, of course, easily said and hugely difficult to do. Many years of negotiation between aboriginals, governments, and the courts will be needed before we can even fully define such claims, let alone resolve them.

Taken together, these assumptions point to a voluntarist solution to the dilemma of the aboriginal peoples. Such a solution would comprise the following steps: All land and other claims for resources against Canada (*not* claims for jurisdiction) should be settled as expeditiously as possible. This could be done by the courts, by negotiation with governments, by a special tribunal or some combination of the above. The important point is to establish the *resources* to which various First Nations are entitled. When this is done, each First Nation leadership would be required to prepare a plan for what I shall call a Talking Circle Society, or TCS,

---

* The argument for this position is implied but not fully explicit in all that I have said so far. This is not the place to present the full argument. It is important, though, to respond to one potential objection: what I propose here ignores the legal rights to self-government now enjoyed by aboriginal peoples and recognized by the courts. In this regard I merely want to note that such an arrangement will prove inherently unstable, because it would offend the basic presuppositions of Canadian society (composed of aboriginals and non-aboriginals), primarily by creating a level of government and a set of rights based on race rather than on our common humanity, and because it runs contrary to the interests of most individual aboriginals themselves. A wise government will seek to extinguish by treaty what has, in most cases, been created by treaty.

a name I borrow from one traditional model of tribal consultation and decision making. Ownership of the resources belonging to the First Nation, would be vested in the TCS. The TCS itself, however, would be owned by all the members of the nation, as equal shareholders.

A plan for corporate bylaws and rules of internal government would be prepared, creating an executive structure and regular accountability to shareholders. In order for the resources to be released to the TCS, a vote of all shareholders would have to be taken, indicating that they agreed with the proposed plan. Without delineating here the method of voting, the principle is that there must be a clear and unambiguous expression of opinion by each individual member of the First Nation (with no arbitrary exclusions), each person counting for one and no more than one vote. Such a plan would have to contain a provision requiring the TCS to purchase from any stockholder his or her shares at fair market value if he or she felt that some other capital investment would produce a better return, if the TCS seemed ill-managed, or if the demands of membership were too onerous or restrictive. The TCS would function as a holding company for the assets of the members of the nation. It could and should, however, play a much greater role in creating the institutions necessary to what we have come to conceive of as aboriginal self-government.

Discussions of aboriginal self-government tend to focus too narrowly on questions of jurisdiction, on whether aboriginal or non-aboriginal *governments* would have the final say in matters directly affecting aboriginal people. My suggestion here is that we vest sovereignty in aboriginal individuals, via the device of the TCS. The aboriginal justice system provides an example of how this might work.

One of the conditions of being a shareholder in the TCS might be that all shareholders must submit all disputes with other shareholders *or* with the TCS itself to binding arbitration in a traditional aboriginal forum. The members of such communities could thereby insulate themselves in the vast majority of cases from the jurisdiction of the ordinary courts merely by agreeing among themselves in advance to do so. There is ample precedent for non-judicial conflict resolution between private parties in our society. As long as share ownership remains voluntary, the requirement for submitting to arbitration remains so as well. The requirement for share repurchase at fair market value protects individuals from manipulation of the share price in order to force them to remain in the community. (Fair market value, in the case of a TCS with 1000 members, might be 1/1000th of the market value of the TCS's total assets.) The ordinary courts would remain open in cases of conflicts between shareholders and outsiders. More importantly, however, since the agreement between shareholders and the TCS is contractual in nature, it remains subject to the oversight role enjoyed by the courts in respect of all contracts, protecting those rights that we as individuals cannot surrender even by freely agreeing to do so.

Health, education, and social services could be provided by the TCS for members who wished them. A capitation system, for example, could be imagined whereby the TCS would receive from government an amount representing the cost of providing such services to the individuals who contract annually with the TCS. Shamans and other traditional spiritual figures could be hired, and sweat lodges could be owned and operated for the members alongside traditional European services.

The TCS could continue, as at present, to manage all tribal assets collectively, by whatever management structure was approved by the shareholders. Such a structure could be occupied by clan mothers, for example. They would not only be answerable to the majority of shareholders, but to individual shareholders as well, who would have the right to claim their stake in cases where the TCS was not meeting their needs or not performing up to expectations.

If, as I expect would be the case, TCSs were incorporated by an act of parliament as part of the final settlement of all claims for land and resources, there could be a third check on the authority of management. If the TCSs were empowered to issue non-voting shares, bonds, and other instruments to raise capital for the members without diluting ownership, the market would also exercise its discipline. Poorly managed TCSs would find it hard to raise capital. Such non-voting shares would provide the perfect avenue for non-aboriginal individuals and organizations who wished to express solidarity and support for the aboriginal communities to do so in the most concrete way possible: by investing their own money in aboriginal endeavours.

While at the outset property ownership would be, as at present, collective, it would also be possible to sell or otherwise transfer TCS assets to members or non-members, so that TCS members could become homeowners on land now belonging to the tribe, build up personal assets (in addition to their voting share in the TCS), and become more easily eligible for commercial loans than at present. It might be a condition of such sales that the TCS be given first refusal if the property went on the market, so as to prevent control of TCS lands passing massively to non-members.

With the resources at its disposal, the TCSs could, if they wished, promote traditional aboriginal ways of life. They could buy fishing quotas, or finance hunting and trapping out of the profits realized from prudent management of their resources. Aboriginal art could be promoted and marketed. A large market would emerge for entrepreneurs in traditional aboriginal skills (language, mediation, healing, spiritual counselling, and so on), who could market their skills to TCSs. TCSs could choose to manage their resources (numbering, in many cases, in the hundreds of millions of dollars) themselves, or hire management firms, or some combination of the two.

TCSs would not, of course, be limited to supporting traditional ways of life. Income from capital or negotiated government grants could be used to promote university education or entrepreneurship in areas deemed important to the community. On the other hand, individuals could be allowed to "borrow" some percentage of the value of their shares to finance educational or business choices not covered by the TCS programs. Such borrowing could be repaid in cash (from businesses) or in kind (as when medical students contract with their TCS to supply medical services to community members for a specified period after completion of their training).

Clearly some method would have to be devised for the transfer of shares between generations. Similarly, the question of allowing compulsory buyouts of shares by the TCS as a method of ostracism would have to be faced, as would the matter of allowing admission to new shareholders (other than direct descendents). Another obvious question would be whether a part of the assets of the TCS could be entailed, guaranteeing that the present generation could not confer on itself too many benefits at the expense of future generations. These are, however, technical questions that pose no insuperable obstacles.

The advantages of such an approach are many. We avoid the sterile debate over jurisdiction between governments by vesting ultimate decision-making power in individual aboriginals. The TCS is an infinitely flexible instrument that gives freely cooperating aboriginals the framework they need to adapt the aboriginal way of life to their own circumstances. The existence of many TCSs would furnish an easy yardstick for aboriginals trying to gauge the performance of their own community, and would encourage experiments in aboriginal living that could be copied by others.

Most importantly for society as a whole, the TCS plan would allow us to realize all these goods without renouncing our commitment to protecting the individual's basic right to his or her own choices about how to live. And most important for aboriginal people in particular, the responsibilities and the rewards pertaining to the survival of aboriginal culture would finally lie with their natural guardians: those individuals who value that culture and wish to devote their efforts to its continued flourishing.

Lament for Leviathan: Our Constitutional Conundrum

And mutual fear brings peace,
Till the selfish love increase;
Then Cruelty knits a snare,
And spreads his baits with care.

He sits down with holy fears,
And waters the ground with tears;
Then Humility takes its root
Underneath his foot.

William Blake, The Human Abstract

THE superiority of Charlottetown over Meech Lake, the earnest young professor from a prairie university said, lay in its "vision." Meech Lake's vision was too narrow, too exclusionary; Charlottetown tried harder to embrace more visions and, therefore, was better, but alas, not yet good enough. There will be no end to our troubles, she seemed to say, until we get everyone's vision of the country and their place in it into the Constitution.

Do Canadians, then, like some American politicians, have trouble with "that vision thing"? Yes, and that trouble is nowhere clearer than in our Mexican standoff on the Constitution. But the conclusion that we need more vision, not less, is precisely the reverse of the truth. Whether we consult our own recent experience or much of Western political tradition, the conclusion is the same. The more we seek to accommodate within the Constitution the various visions people may have of the country, the more we will tear this country apart.

I will try to flesh out this argument here, taking as a starting point an interpretation of the political significance of the three most recent attempts at comprehensive constitutional reform: the Trudeau round, the Meech Lake round, and the Canada round. Such reflection may lead to a fresh appreciation of the neglected wisdom of Western constitutional thought.

My intepretation of recent attempts at constitutional reform (one successful, two not), is simplified and condensed here as a series of statements focusing exclusively on the role that competing visions — and reactions to such visions — have played in those attempts: visions of what Canada is now, visions of the relative importance of certain groups within society, and visions of a desirable future. This is not to suggest that other matters have not played a key role in the unfolding of our constitutional affairs, but merely that we have never properly taken measure of the role of vision in understanding our present impasse.

The picture I have in mind looks like this. In 1982, the Constitution was changed. The old Constitution comprised two principal elements: individual Canadians inhabiting largely undifferentiated territorial communities (provinces) and living under a regime both federal and parliamentary. But 1982 extended that basic model by granting formal constitutional status to a number of individual rights enjoyed by all Canadians. Onto that simple model, however, was also grafted a new vision of a Canada composed of certain named groups (for example, women, the disabled, aboriginal peoples, multicultural groups, speakers of official languages), who had certain characteristics and were to enjoy certain rights. This raised enormously the constitutional stakes for Quebec's political elite, who had invested twenty-five years of political capital in arguing the distinctiveness of that province's society relative to English-speaking Canada. Now, not only was that elite's notion of Quebec's place in Canada not reflected in the current constitutionally endorsed one, but new groups had achieved constitutional status and recognition of their special needs and rights. Only a constitutional embrace of a vision of the province's distinctiveness, we were assured, could dissuade Quebec from quitting the country. Enter Meech Lake.

Predictably, the embodiment in the Meech Lake Accord of one of Quebec's visions of its place in Canada created new grievances, such as when residents of the Territories and members of French-language minorities *hors Québec* felt that this new vision made them "second-class citizens." On the other side, groups whose demands were to some extent met in 1982 (women, multicultural groups, and native peoples, to cite but three) felt that their gains would be downgraded because *their* vision of *their* place in Canada would lose the prestige and cachet of being singled out for explicit constitutional recognition. And the coup de grâce was delivered when English Canada interpreted Bill 178 as a foretaste of distinctiveness to come. *Exeunt* Meech.

To counter these alleged reasons for the failure of Meech, the Canada Clause was at the centre of the next attempt to square our constitutional circle: the Charlottetown Accord. The purpose of this clause was, in part at least, to give a stake in constitutional reform to groups previously outside the charmed circle; trade unionists, Quebeckers, visible minorities, and others were wooed with a constitutional baptism, while others had their constitutional naming reaffirmed. Again, however, some groups (for example, the National Action Committee on the Status of Women and the disabled) nevertheless persisted in feeling that the previously strong currency of their constitutional recognition was being debased.

New attempts to embrace aboriginal visions through a constitutional right to self-government gave rise to new resistance from aboriginal women, who saw with a jaundiced eye traditional male-dominated aboriginal society. Many Westerners — despite attempts to "compensate" them with Senate reform — could not rid themselves of the fear that distinctiveness for Quebec and self-government for aboriginals meant inferior constitutional status (and probably higher taxes) for themselves. Finally, feeling that the importance and status of distinct society was too watered down by the Canada Clause, Senate reform, and the recognition of an extensive constitutional special status for aboriginals, Quebec followed the rest of the country in rejecting Charlottetown. So many visions, so little agreement.

What this thumbnail (and slightly caricatured) sketch does is suggest a wholly different interpretation of our constitutional fixation and its consequences from those offered by the vision merchants. This latter group blithely claims that constitutional reform will succeed only when we have sufficiently opened up the Constitution to enough visions and carefully balanced these against one another.

The failures of Meech and Charlottetown are not isolated incidents, and neither was, nor could have been, a one-off round of negotiations to complete what was started by Trudeau in 1981. In fact, Meech and Charlottetown pursue (and starkly illustrate) a line of thought that was already foreshadowed in the Constitution Act (1867), but only became fully established for the first time in our Constitution by the Trudeau package of reforms. The result of this change has been, and will continue to be, an endless series of constitutional quarrels, each one serving not to strengthen but to rend the country's constitutional fabric.

What was done in 1981–82 fundamentally changed the relation of each Canadian to the Constitution. Some have suggested that the change provides a vision to draw the country together, a "nationally integrating" set of values (via a universal set of rights embodied in the Charter), values to which we can all give our allegiance. In seeking to define the significance of Trudeau's reforms, it is right to focus on vision and values, but wrong to believe that the ones that were inserted will draw the nation together. On the contrary, our Constitution now saddles us with a number of values or visions (the terms are essentially interchangeable here) that threaten both the country and some of our most cherished beliefs. To see why, it may be helpful to reflect on the nature of visions and values.

THE PROBLEM ON WHICH WE NEED to focus our attention arises as soon as we introduce this concept of "value." The things we value are the things we find good, worthy, desirable, and so on. But it is a commonplace of the Western liberal democratic tradition that values are highly personal, that the worth of particular values cannot, for instance, be established scientifically or objectively.

A belief in God, the inviolability of Nature, or the overriding importance of peace may all be laudable in themselves, and opposition to them may be ill advised or shortsighted, but these are ideas whose moral value depends on our individual endorsement of and attachment to them. Precisely this truth finally defeated the Inquisition of the Middle Ages: its powers could only ever enforce external observance of the forms of religion, whereas what must matter in God's eyes is the state of the soul, the presence or absence of belief and faith. True belief and faith are the products of free will.

So values are a wholly different matter than, say, our understanding of the physical world. We can fairly say that someone who refuses to recognize that he or she is bound by the law of gravity is acting irrationally is refusing to recognize the objective and demonstrable nature of the world. Some of our fashionable but overwrought philosophers of science may try to deny that there is such an objectivity to the physical world, and from a philosophical point of view they may be right. But from a practical point of view, these same philosophers expect their lights to go on when they flip the switch and are annoyed when they don't. There simply are regularities of behaviour about the physical world on which we can count (although our explanations of those regularities may prove wrong), and there are statements about the physical world that are demonstrably wrong: the world is not flat and the sun does not revolve around the Earth. And while it certainly is true that our beliefs influence our understanding of the physical world, our beliefs do not determine what the physical world does; all the philosophers of science in the world could sign a solemn statement that water should boil at 110 degrees Celsius at sea level and it would change nothing. When we talk about the right way to live, though, there is no such rationally compelling evidence available to refute those who refuse to subscribe to our beliefs about most of what we call values.

If we are right in thinking that there is no ground available for choosing objectively between different values, between the different things that people find good and set for themselves as goals or objectives in life, then the choice of what values we are to pursue cannot be the business of government. If all choices are equally value-laden and equally incapable of objective demonstration, then those chosen by elected officials, or even those chosen by a majority of electors, must always remain arbitrary choices; there can be little moral justification for forcing them on people who disagree with them.

Critics on the cultural Right will attempt (wrongly) to attribute to me the absurd view that there is nothing that can be said in favour of or against particular choices about how to live (thus raising the dreaded spectre of "value relativism"). I am merely underlining the pointlessness of using the coercive machinery of the state to enforce any group's or individual's choices in this regard. There are many social and other mechanisms that will work to weed out some choices, by showing them to be less desirable than others. Countless occupations, religions, and family structures have been tried by different people at different times but have not spread, because their benefits were few, their costs many. They withered and died.

Yet those constant "experiments in living" (to use John Stuart Mills's happy phrase) are indispensable for at least two reasons. The first has been well explained by such modern philosophers of science as Sir Karl Popper. Our knowledge is always fallible, so our beliefs about the world must always be held to be *provisional,* subject to constant revision as our understanding of the world becomes more sophisticated. The picture of the atomic and sub-atomic world that I was taught in school is now regarded as laughably primitive and misleading; we might, however, still be stuck with it if some government power had dictated that it be enforced as the final incorrigible truth and punished scientists who tried to prove otherwise. Free experiments in living serve both to open new vistas of human endeavour and happiness *and* to reaffirm the relative success of a society's traditions. If our way of life is, in fact, the best way to reach human happiness and fulfillment, as cultural conservatives claim, how can this be substantiated except by letting that way of life compete with alternatives? Competition between traditions, and a weighing of the (always provisional) results, is how we discover the balance of advantages and disadvantages of particular forms of life.

Experiments in living find their second justification in a reason that goes beyond the analogy with knowledge of the physical world. Unlike, say, atoms, which cannot modify their behaviour on the basis of experience, human beings can modify theirs, as any economist can demonstrate. We may never understand fully the laws that govern the actions of atoms, but we understand the constants of their behaviour well enough to be able to manipulate them predictably with stunning practical consequences. People, on the other hand, are constantly altering their behaviour as they discover new things about themselves, and as technology and other developments make possible what had previously only been dreams. We are, therefore, not justified in using a historical pattern of human flourishing as grounds for coercing people to conform to that pattern. We do not, and probably never will, know the directions in which the potentialities of the human spirit can lead us. We are not yet all that we may be.

This view of relations between individuals within society does not deny that there must be rules of acceptable behaviour that will be enforced by the courts; we could not live together and benefit from all the advantages that cooperation with others procures for us without rules against murder, violence, fraud, theft, rules of the road, rules about what we can do with our waste. But to be consistent with the notion of the subjective nature of human values, such rules must not seek to impose a preferred way of life, nor to lay down or define the "right way to live." On the contrary, they must attempt to define and proscribe only those ways of pursuing our own values (whatever they may be) that are not consistent with our sharing a society with others who are also pursuing their values. The rules must not be concerned with the values themselves.

Such laws are like signposts telling us what routes are available to us to reach our destination, indicating where we can turn left or right, when we must yield to others on the road, and when we have the right of way. But these rules do not try to impose on us a view of which is the "good" or "best" destination. Such rules are necessary for all of us to make use of society's rich and dense network of resources and knowledge to achieve our own purposes without harming others who are trying to do the same thing. The rules are designed to minimize conflict between users who are not pursuing the same ends and, therefore, can only be led to cooperate by rules that maximize access.

While this may describe an ideal state of affairs in liberal democratic society, we have never been able to realize fully such a set of rules in practice. One of the principal reasons for this is that governments have been all too willing to use the coercive power of the state to protect or promote the interests or values of powerful

Brian Lee Crowley

groups or individuals. This sometimes takes the form of artificial monopolies created by laws protecting certain producers; in Canada we have only to think of the various telephone and hydro companies, or of the so-called self-governing professions like lawyers, doctors, dentists, or trade unionists — all of whom use powers conferred on them by the state to restrict artificially the supply of their services and thus raise their income.

Sometimes, too, governments have permitted themselves the luxury of skewing the rules in favour of members of particular groups, instead of trying to arrive at rules that treat all individuals as persons of equal worth regardless of their values or their membership (by mere accident of birth or choice) in some group, be it linguistic, racial, social, or sexual. Think of apartheid in South Africa, special privileges for the *nomenklatura* in communist states, and here in Canada reverse discrimination in favour of such disadvantaged groups as racial minorities or women.

Recognizing that the power of government can be abused, the Western liberal political tradition has always made an important place for *constitutionalism,* the doctrine that it ought not to be left to the whim of rulers to decide how and in whose favour their power ought to be exercised, but that rules ought to be laid down about the legitimate uses to which such power may be put. An important part of the struggle for constitutionalism was the belief that, since all people are equal, they all ought to have an equal say in the choice of political leaders, and political power ought not to be monopolized by some particular class. Democracy, it was hoped, would usher in an era in which all would be free under impartial laws applied equally to each, and in which political power would not be abused since it would be controlled by the people who had to live under it.

The architects of modern liberal democracy have sometimes forgotten or overlooked the fact that majorities, too, can misuse their political power if that power is not also subjected to rules — not just about procedure, but about substance. There is, after all,

114

a world of difference between the formal democratic principle that people should only be subject to laws of which at least a majority approves, and the substantive principle, which holds that anything that has majority approval will make good law.

THIS MIGHT BE ONE REASON to think that the 1982 constitutional reform was a step in the direction of a greater liberalization of Canada's political institutions. After all, it added the Charter of Rights and Freedoms, whose putative role is to protect individuals from improper attempts by governments to interfere in their private choices. If the reform had stopped there, it might have been such an improvement, although abstract constitutional statements of rights, ripped from their concrete context, have always evoked in me grave misgivings; the price we paid for patriation in terms of political and institutional disruption was far too high relative to the meagre benefits. Far worse than these drawbacks, however, is the ambivalent view of rights at the heart of the Charter itself. Not only does it confer rights on individuals, but it singles out members of specific groups for some form of special recognition or extended rights flowing from their identification with such groups (for example, "aboriginal peoples," the "socially or the economically disadvantaged," groups promoting "multiculturalism," and groups that are disadvantaged "because of race, national or ethnic origin, colour, religion, sex, age or mental or physical disability").

The 1982 reform doesn't just try to set a neutral framework within which all Canadians can make their own choices about their lives (those decisions taken as a whole representing what Canada is at any one moment). Instead it tries to state a vision of what Canada is and to fix that vision in the Constitution, a vision involving a Canada composed of specified groups, exhibiting features that are held to be in some sense an eternal essence of the country. Whether or not we agree with these values (and I and many other Canadians do happen to agree with many of them) is not at issue. What *is* at issue is whether or not the Constitution is the proper place to put them.

To see what is at stake in this question, one needs to consider afresh the notions of vision and values. There are two principles on which cooperation between people can be based. The first is that they can agree on ends or values that they have in common and that they decide to pursue in concert; the shared commitment to a goal, then, makes individuals acquiesce in the assignment of particular tasks and the distribution of available resources by the recognized leaders in the group. If the players on the Montreal Canadiens want to play good hockey, they can't each decide for themselves individually what positions they're going to play, how much time they're going to spend on the ice, or what plays they are going to make. For the group to reach its chosen goal, there must be captains, coaches, trainers, and managers who make decisions about how each member of the team can make their most effective contribution.

The second way to make cooperation between people possible is to seek agreement not on visions or values, but on the forms of behaviour each of us will observe if left alone to pursue our own values as we see them. This harks back to the example of the rules of the road; we do not need to agree on where each of us should be going to agree to cooperate in the use of the streets. The idea here is that if you follow the same impersonal rules as everyone else, no one is allowed to interfere in your use of the public highway to go wherever you please.

Team-style cooperation is based on a substantive agreement on what is good (we are here to play good hockey). Rules-of-the-road-style cooperation rests on a procedural agreement on what is just or fair (we are traveling to self-chosen destinations for our own private reasons, but we can see the need to cooperate with others on fair procedures if all of us are to reach these destinations safely).

The first principle has an important deficiency as a principle of overarching political cooperation. A political society is different from other organizations — a hockey team, a corporation, a trade union — because membership in it is not optional; if one inhabits the national territory, one belongs automatically, and the obligations of membership are enforced by law. Given the subjective nature of values, there is no reason to suppose that all citizens, thrown together by fate and the caprices of geography, will share the same values. Even in the unlikely event that they do, such a consensus can be no more than a temporary coincidence. This must mean that attempts to embody concrete goals (other than the maintenance of the universal and impersonal rules of social cooperation themselves) in the law is to treat those people who disagree with such values as *things*. Individuals become objects to be manipulated for the purposes of public policy, and the values or visions that underpin the policies are given special status without moral or rational ground.

TWO SOLUTIONS TO THIS DILEMMA present themselves. Faced with what the moral philosopher Isaiah Berlin has called the "irreducible plurality of values," we can seek to open up the Constitution to as wide a range of value-statements or visions as possible. On this view, since there is no "right" vision of Canada, we should put as many of them as possible into our fundamental law, so that no one (or at least no one who swings important political weight) feels left out.

This was one prominent commentator's defence of the Meech Lake Accord: having admitted in 1981–82 the principle of constitutional visions, the only fair thing to do is to have a lot of them. It was certainly the inspiration of the so-called Canada Clause in the Charlottetown Accord, which tried to give a nod in the direction of a number of values important to most political or morally powerful groups in the country at the moment. The Canada Clause gave comfort to many groups who had found Meech myopic as a "vision thing" statement.

The absurdity of this position is almost immediately apparent. As soon as one admits that values are subjective and that they belong in the Constitution, there is no rational or moral ground on which we can exclude any value whatsoever. We have not fully understood the direction that this takes us, for the authors and critics of Meech and Charlottetown assumed that the problem to be confronted was deciding *whose* vision to include. We have not yet grasped that the real problem is that *any* such choice is a choice to exclude other visions. Yet any attempt to exclude particular values must appear to those who hold them as an indefensible and arbitrary act of will by government or political majorities. The logical conclusion must be that the Constitution itself becomes a new apple of discord, an object of perpetual contention as long as every group and individual with strong feelings about some aspect of their way of life feels that this value has not received the constitutional sanction to which it is entitled.

The consequences of this conclusion are far-reaching. In a system in which such demands can be and are granted, every particular group must organize and press its demands for recognition on government or suffer the ignominious fate of being relegated to the status of second-class citizens, people whose constitutional machismo is threatened by their so far unsuccessful attempts to obtain the sort of symbolic sanction and recognition that entrenchment provides. Of course, this struggle for constitutional recognition of groups is merely a particular instance of a larger political problem of Western democracies: almost everyone is organized in some group for the purpose of extorting from government whatever benefit they think they are worthy of, these claims being backed up by the threat of withdrawal of electoral support. Benefits are granted to particular groups, not because of the intrinsic worth of the claim, but because of the purely contingent fact that at a given moment they are believed by politicians to have the power to make or break "coalition builders" seeking to make or break an electoral majority.

This way of putting the problem we face is intentionally redolent of the thought of one of the greatest (and most misunderstood) political thinkers of European tradition: Thomas Hobbes. This is not the place for a treatise on political thought, but I invoked Hobbes's masterpiece in this essay's title because the argument so far amounts to the claim that we have forgotten or never really learned two Hobbesian truths. For this neglect of our own tradition we are paying a high price.

The first Hobbesian lesson is simply the recognition of the relativity of human attainments and status, as well as their ephemeral nature. People are rarely content to judge their lot in absolute terms, but seek always comparison with others. A man content with his salary can be made immediately miserable on learning that his colleague earns more. Many a child's school years have been made wretched, not because their academic performance was poor, but because their parents discovered it was less distinguished than that of the neighbours' or relatives' children. A great deal of human happiness flows from our status relative to others. Constitutionally, this means that we cannot take the acceptance of the status quo by some as a sign that they will acquiesce in changes demanded by others who find the current arrangements unsatisfactory. On the contrary, if the changes are believed to confer new status (distinctiveness or group rights or affirmation of worth) on some groups, this alone will create new frictions between groups and will create *new* demands for constitutional recognition from groups once content not to be specified in the Constitution.

The second Hobbesian lesson, then, is that if anyone gets special status or recognition, everyone will feel entitled to it and demand it. The result: a spiraling growth in conflict that undermines the authority of the state, and the destruction of the peace and stability desired by every member of the community.

Hobbes saw with characteristic clarity that the best solution for imperfect human beings like ourselves is the rule of law, where *all* are subject to the same rules of community life, with no arbitrary distinctions between persons on the basis of their membership in this or that group. Added to this is the insight that law is best confined to those rules essential for peaceful coexistence. Distinctiveness or cultural difference, or whatever else may distinguish people from one another, should be neither created nor denied by political institutions, for this undermines belief in the neutrality of those institutions, which is the sole guarantor of peace.

TO ILLUSTRATE, IT MIGHT HELP to start with a fascinating *non-constitutional* example: the decision several years ago to allow Sikh RCMP constables to wear turbans. Under the cloak of "multiculturalism," this decision granted the peculiar principle that religious conviction warrants individual RCMP officers to display their private beliefs in the course of carrying out their public duties. Having admitted the principle and allowed Sikhs to wear turbans, the RCMP immediately found themselves in the position of trying to refuse the demand of aboriginal constables to wear traditional braids. Other similar demands for new dispensations are sure to follow.

The distinction between "tradition" and "religion" on which the RCMP based their ruling on the aboriginal request seems improper; it requires public authorities to decide what is important to particular individuals' identities. Only two rules would seem morally defensible in that they do not require us to make such essentially contestable distinctions between people and their visions: either one uniform for all, or all variations desired by constables themselves. Anything else would be mere fiat.

The popular notion that the turban controversy was about freedom-of-religion is simply wrong. Seeing why it's wrong is important in helping us to choose between the two rules just outlined. This choice is all about the place of private values in the public domain; how we understand and answer questions like this one will tell us a great deal about our chances for constitutional peace.

The freedom-of-religion approach relies on the fact that conscientious Sikhs must wear turbans. Turbans were not allowed by the RCMP dress code, *ergo* the code was exclusionary; its vision was too limited, it discriminated against people with a certain set of beliefs, with a different vision. From another vantage point, however, the matter seems much less clear-cut. The devout of each religion have activities from which they must abstain because those activities offend the way of life ordained for them by their deity. The pious Catholic will not work in an abortion clinic any more than the deeply religious Jew could accept a job requiring him to work on Saturdays, or than a devout Muslim could be a bacon-taster in a meat-packing plant. This is not discrimination against them. There is simply an incompatibility between certain choices open to such individuals. They cannot choose both and remain true to their beliefs.

The existence of such an incompatibility *would* give rise to discrimination in one set of circumstances. If the incompatibility were created *for the purpose* of excluding people with certain beliefs, and had no other justification apart from such an exclusion, then we would be faced with improper discrimination. So each case of such conflicts must be examined on its merits. We appear to have such a conflict in the case of turbaned aspirants to membership in the RCMP. But the rule imposing a uniform (and the word is well chosen) was instituted long before the notion of Sikh applicants even arose. What *is* the rationale for a uniform?

The purpose of the uniform — perhaps paradoxically — is indispensable in a multicultural society. It emphasizes the distinction between a social role (in this case that of agent of public order) and the person who fills that role. The message sent out by constables' uniform appearance is that all constables, regardless of their private beliefs and commitments, are held to a uniform code of behaviour, that when they don the uniform, they agree to put aside their personal preferences and apply a uniform code of justice to one and all. Failure to do so is properly a serious breach of discipline.

This clear distinction between role and person, between office and private beliefs, is even more essential in a society composed of members of many cultures, for all people cannot be expected to conform to an underlying set of cultural beliefs. When such a widespread set of beliefs exists it can often be more effective in maintaining public order than the police can ever be. In a multicultural society with widely varying assumptions about right and wrong, the police, to be effective, must not have, and must be seen not to have, any *parti pris* between the members of different cultures who are likely to be parties to disputes. When an individual feels that his or her private beliefs, religious or otherwise, cannot be subordinated to the requirements of uniformity that accompany the social role of police officer, there are strong grounds for wondering whether the first commitment is to the private beliefs or to the social role. That in itself would be grounds for excluding such people from service in the forces of public order. This would not be a violation of freedom of conscience. No one is forced by law to be an RCMP officer; the choice of a way of life is entirely open. What the law and individual rights cannot ignore is the fact that some choices are incompatible, and free individuals must live with the consequences, joys, and disappointments of their choices and commitments.

Even more important than this ground for refusing deviations from the uniform code, however, is the changed perception of the police that such behaviour is likely to work in the public mind. Remember that the principle admitted by the RCMP is that sincere religious belief warrants relaxation of the uniform discipline. We can be certain that this principle will be extended far beyond its first application, and that the aboriginal demand for similar recognition is only the second of many sallies to enlarge this freshly opened breach.

Consider the consequences. Will drunken brawlers on St. Patrick's Day welcome the intervention of a policeman wearing his Orange Order sash? Will constables of religions requiring them to proselytize be permitted to hand out tracts with traffic tickets? Are many feminists likely to regard the veil of a Muslim female constable as a sign of someone sympathetic to their interests? What must concern us in each of these hypothetical instances is that public confidence in the impartiality of the police, and in their ability to apply the law evenhandedly, would be seriously undermined. In a multicultural society in which there are many conflicts between cultures, deviations from uniformity are invitations to see the police as representatives of one side or the other, rather than as neutral third parties.

I SUGGESTED EARLIER that this digression was relevant to the Constitution. The link comes through the distinction between role or office on the one hand, and private belief on the other. One of the roles individuals play is that of citizen. The problem is how far the Constitution should go in recognizing the personal or private identities of citizens.

A constitution is supposed to comprise the rules of the political game. People are only likely to play a game if they know in advance what the rules are, and if they are convinced that those rules make no arbitrary distinctions between players. When the rules are seen as fair in this way, the players accept that it will be unpredictable combinations of skill and luck that produce winners and losers.

But imagine for a moment what would happen if the rules had to include a statement of belief about the relative importance of particular *groups* of players, and if those statements were only satisfactory when they corresponded to each group's own evaluation of their importance, rather than some disinterested evaluation. The game would rapidly grind to a halt as players refused to play under such intolerable conditions. Add to this the certainty that groups who have already obtained recognition will resist extension of similar recognition to others on the grounds that this implies a relative diminution of their own (no doubt not yet fully satisfactory) status, and we have a fairly good representation of the bad-tempered debate that surrounded both the Meech Lake and Charlottetown accords. It certainly corresponds to the account I gave of that debate at the beginning of this essay.

Both to clarify the argument and to prevent misunderstanding, it may be worthwhile for me to nail my own colours to the mast here. I am firmly of the view that if values of this sort are to be placed in the Constitution, if statements are to be made about the relative merits of various groups, as opposed to either silence or a fundamental statement about the equal worth of all Canadians, then Quebec's demand for recognition as a distinct society is a reasonable one and ought to be granted. At the same time, I think it unreasonable to grant the same recognition to all the other provinces, because there is no justification for many of them to have powers to which I believe Quebec alone has a legitimate claim.

But I have equally come to the view that since I am not prepared to agree to all the possible constitutional visions of Canada, and since I am also forced to admit that all such substantive visions (including, naturally, my own) are based on values about which people of good faith can disagree, the only reasonable solution is a rule that no such visions be allowed in the Constitution, including the ones in which I am in full or partial agreement. This is precisely the conclusion to which Hobbes thinks reasonable people will be led by the intractable nature of social conflict.

Our constitutional dilemma admits only two possible solutions: one illusory, the other practical and durable. The illusory one is to include *everyone's* vision. This is impossible, not least because the visions of some are so offensive to others that we could never reach agreement, and the attempt to do so would alienate many, as Meech and Charlottetown have illustrated. The practical solution is to renounce substantive visions altogether and just let Canadians get on with the business of defining Canada for themselves in their minds and in their actions.

The advantage of the latter solution is that it allows the peaceful coexistence of every possible vision of the country. It provides that rarest of political prizes: a framework within which no one, including government, may prevent you or anyone else from living whatever life you like, subject to the requirement of reciprocal abstinence from demonstrable harm. No one is excluded, belittled, rejected, or offended, because every choice of a way of life, every community, every idea of what Canada is and can be is recognized implicitly but solidly in the still and quiet air of a delightful constitutional silence.

THERE IS A FURTHER ASPECT to the folly of trying to give appropriate constitutional recognition to visions and groups. That is the hubristic belief that people at any given moment in the history of a society of free people can or should make statements about their own self-understandings that will be binding on their successors, who may (and almost certainly *will*) be different kinds of people. Yet this is exactly what we do when we entrench these values, because, as the Meech Lake and Charlottetown architects discovered to their chagrin, the written constitution is designed intentionally to be very difficult to change. This is for sound reasons: the rules are designed to provide a general framework within which politicians and political majorities must work if their decisions are to meet basic standards of decency and fairness. If politicians could simply ignore or change the rules when they became inconvenient, they would no longer be a rampart against abuse of power or against the temptation to break the general rules of acceptable behaviour to achieve particular purposes that seem desirable in themselves.

This shows the remarkable insight of the description of the American Constitution by one of its authors as an appeal from the people sober to the people drunk. This document represented the best efforts of the American founding fathers to set out rules of political behaviour in a calm, reflective way, without any particular policy objectives in mind; to define, in other words, political means that can defensibly be used by majorities in pursuit of their aims.

The importance of such a set of rules is quickly revealed by reflecting on our own tendency to bend the rules of decent social behaviour to get things we strongly desire. The social and religious taboo against adultery is all too easily swept aside by passion, while Rambo and the Terminator continually lend credence to the fantastic belief that violence is the only means of dealing with those who stop us from getting what we want. To recognize temptation in ourselves is to recognize it in politicians: when they are in hot pursuit of a particular goal in which they believe, and have the support of the electorate, they are often tempted to use ill considered or inappropriate means to reach that goal. Constitutionalism aims at preventing the regret that often arises the morning after such binges of self-indulgence.

We must never lose sight, however, of the fact that the whole justification of constitutionalism's rules is that they are rules of fair procedure; they set out the standards that the political process must respect if its decisions and actions — based on the values of the majority of the moment — are not to overstep their proper bounds in a society of free people. To put the values of the passing majority themselves into the Constitution, from which they are virtually impossible to remove, holds future generations hostage to another era. It is only in this latter context that the old maxim "Constitutions give dead men votes" has any force.

The Constitution Act (1867) provides a good example of this

stumbling block. In it, certain (primarily educational) rights are recognized for Protestants and Catholics. Not rights for those who profess any set of beliefs, not rights for all citizens regardless of their beliefs, but rights for those who profess certain beliefs. This has long been considered a major obstacle to modernizing the Quebec school system, where the old constitutionally protected confessional divide prevents a reorganization in accordance with modern linguistic self-definitions. More obviously, it has been a cause of some resentment among Jews in Quebec, for example, who must either send their children to private Hebrew schools or to the publicly funded Protestant system.

Similarly, in Ontario, Jewish and other groups are continuing their legal challenge of provincial funding of Catholic separate schools on the grounds that the provision of funding for only one group outside the public system is incompatible with Charter guarantees of equality. So far the courts have found that the guarantee of confessional rights in 1867 was part of the original confederal bargain and so remained untouched by the Charter. This turns the values of another generation into a straitjacket for us today. If we were starting afresh we might all be able to agree either that all denominations should receive equal funding or that there should be a single public system that takes no account of such matters. I suspect, however, that there would be little support for the current constitutionally entrenched values, even by many who consider themselves Protestant or Catholic.

The moral here is that in a society where people are left to make their own decisions about who they are and who they want to become, a society that is open to newcomers and new ideas and influences, as well as to the self-transformations of which we and our progeny are all capable, it is the height of presumption for one generation to assume that what it finds good will be found good, or even intelligible, by those in the future.

The 1981 constitutional reforms were forged at a time when groups of people defined themselves primarily as women (as distinct from men), as aboriginal people (as distinct from whites), as francophones (as distinct from allophones and anglophones), and were powerful enough to get some form of special constitutional recognition for these self-definitions and for these particular social conflicts. But just as the Protestant–Catholic conflict and self-definition has been displaced by these (and others), these newer ones, too, can and will be superseded or transformed as we and those who come after us change the ways we see ourselves.

Who is to say that in twenty-five or fifty years the chief social and political conflicts in this country will not be between Northerners and Southerners, between AIDS sufferers and non-AIDS sufferers, between nature-starved city dwellers and intensive farmers and loggers, or between a rising population living on tax-financed pensions and a shrinking tax-paying population? More fancifully, what if an ecological disaster or some accident of genetic engineering creates a group of mutants who can only live in an environment that would be poisonous to people like ourselves? Conflicts like these could well cut across the groups receiving constitutional recognition today in such a way as to permit particular minorities, arbitrarily defined by us in 1981–82, to have a veto in the future on social changes that may be crucial to ways of life we can only dimly envisage — if we can imagine them at all. It is, after all, just such arbitrarily defined minorities in Quebec and Ontario that have blocked the emergence of a school system that would be a true reflection of a profoundly different society from that of 1867.

Unlike one's religious faith, though, one cannot change one's sex or race, so perhaps the comparison is not a fair one. Two replies can be made to this, aside from the obvious one that in these days of genetic engineering and sex-change operations, we should be less quick to leap to conclusions about the immutability of nature.

The first reply is simply to say that each generation naturally believes its preoccupations are the proper preoccupations of the human race throughout time and across nations. An effort of imagination is needed to project oneself into the mindset and historical circumstances of others one has not known personally. The Canadians of 1867 were, no doubt, just as convinced of the enduring nature of their problems and preoccupations as we are about our own. Moreover, they would have been unlikely to admit the possibility that their descendants would be different in any important way from themselves.

The second reply is that we are not talking about the permanent facts of human existence in the abstract, but about the permanent facts of human existence as they are interpreted, valued, and understood by a particular generation of people. The Catholic–Protestant divide is less important today not because there are no longer Protestants and Catholics, but because these aspects of our identity now have less of a hold on us, and we are freer to distance ourselves from them. We have reached a *modus vivendi* among ourselves about how to handle these differences, and so they recede in importance while others take their place.

The same will happen, in due course, not to the differences between the sexes or races, but to the significance we attach to these matters *in defining who we are*. The relevance of this in the constitutional debate is easily illustrated by the reluctance of feminist groups in Quebec to endorse the English-speaking feminists' opposition to Meech Lake. Hard choices had to be made, in this case in Quebec, about which aspect of one's identity was to carry the day.

Hard as it may be for us to imagine now that those who follow us will have their own neuroses, their own insecurities, their own battles to fight, their own conflicts to resolve. We should be mature enough not to saddle them with ours in addition because we are so full of ourselves as to believe that we represent the culmination of human history and development. Appeals to use the Constitution as a prop for particular cultures and languages and ways of life are all very well, and there is certainly value in cherishing what the past has handed on to us. At least as important in the long run, however, is the mirror opposite of this principle: that the door must be left wide open to new cultures, new forms of life, which we can only dimly imagine, and which do not yet have their defenders. The past must not have a veto on the future.

AN AMBIGUITY OF PURPOSE infused the Constitution in 1867. In 1982, Trudeau's reforms turned that old Victorian crossroad into a modern highway junction, widening and improving the pavement in every direction. But, sadly, no matter how well the roads are engineered, trying to go in two directions at once gets us nowhere. Even the guarantee in the Charter that perhaps should do most to gladden the hearts of liberal democrats and individualists, the one that should be the greatest bulwark against arbitrary treatment and favouritism, is Janus-faced: Section 15, the equality guarantee.

Liberal apologists for 1982 see this section as fundamentally guaranteeing individual equality. To the extent that groups figure in Section 15, it is merely as a part of a larger commitment to achieve equality before and under the law for individual members of these groups, many of whose members have suffered and continue to suffer unfair treatment precisely because of their membership in such groups. One only has to think of the findings of the Marshall inquiry for this to become clear. What's going on is arguably more properly seen not as special treatment for particular groups, but as the identification of particular groups whose members may need to avail themselves of these guarantees.

This argument is superficially tempting but nevertheless mistaken. It overlooks the constitutional approval given to reverse discrimination (affirmative action) in order to redress differences in treatment meted out to particular groups — differences that can only be revealed by statistics that cannot, in themselves, demonstrate the presence or absence of arbitrary discdiminatory treatment of specific individuals.*

---

* See my essay on employment equity in this collection.

But it's not just a question of an optional right of governments to pursue affirmative action. Clearly, the courts feel that the language and intent of Section 15 licenses attempts to achieve group parity or equality. The very wording of the section invites comparisons between groups in determining whether inequality exists; its interpretation is often based on a comparison of the statistically revealed treatment of particular groups. The Supreme Court of Canada has even established a standard of comparison for making such determinations: "similarly situated groups."

This notion of group equality is incompatible with the notions of the rule of law and equality on which liberal democracy is founded. A discussion of the full definition of these three terms (democracy, the rule of law, and equality) is a huge undertaking that exceeds the space available here. A brief sketch of the three main pathways down which that discussion might advance is, nevertheless, worth attempting:

1) Democracy is a method for resolving political disputes, not an end in itself, not a culture, not a set of policy objectives. For democracy to exist there must be political liberty and, therefore, equality of political rights, but nothing in that argument commits one to the view that democracy is precluded or nullified by the existence of important material or other inequalities.

Any discussion about substantive equality is, therefore, a discussion about the *ends* (or values) that a democratic political society ought to pursue. No agreement on democracy as a *means* for resolving disputes about what ends political society ought to pursue requires one to endorse this sort of equality. It is perfectly consistent to be a democrat and to oppose this notion of equality, and yet the language of Section 15 and the practice of its interpretation tends to suggest that if we are a democracy we must be committed, at least, to pursue such equality. This sleight of hand should be resisted.

Brian Lee Crowley

2) Statistical inequalities between, say, the distribution of jobs or incomes between sexes or racial groups can be, at best, tenuous and indirect indicators of discriminatory treatment for individual members of so-called underrepresented groups. But the evil that must be combated is not the statistical inequality between *groups*, but the unequal treatment given for arbitrary reasons to particular *individuals*.

Reverse discrimination is the refuge of those who cannot demonstrate unjust treatment of individuals (which should be the province of the courts and the law), but who want to redress abstract statistical differences between groups on the grounds that, if these differences exist, they must be due to discrimination; and that in a good or desirable society there is an equal distribution of (at least some) desired things across particular groups. But these grounds are patently false, not least because they assume there must be an equal or identical distribution of interests, talents, knowledge, and desires across arbitrarily defined groups, an assumption that is merely taken as an article of faith. In the absence of a convincing demonstration of discrimination against individuals, the differences in statistical distribution represent merely the contingent aggregate of individual choices and nothing more can be said about them. If individuals in their choices of jobs, universities, professions, and so forth are subject to colour-blind or sex-blind admission criteria (and the definition of these is always subject to improvement), in other words, if *individuals* are not treated unjustly or arbitrarily, then how can we go back and describe the overall pattern of such transactions as unjust?

A policy of liberal equality and the rule of law requires us to work at perfecting the rules of procedure (not distribution) so that individuals who compete for jobs, scholarships, and so forth feel that they have been treated fairly (that is, non-arbitrarily) in decision-making. If evidence of discrimination is uncovered, this is the only morally defensible way of dealing with it, the only way that treats all individuals as ends in themselves and not as things to be used by policymakers for their own purposes. Once the rules are fair and non-discriminatory, there can be no further ground for complaint on the basis of aggregates.

To go beyond this is to begin to combat not discrimination, but the choices that other individuals make, on the grounds that they *should* have chosen differently, or because they *might* have chosen differently if the social order had been different. But the view that some other pattern of choices or some other form of social order is itself desirable is a quite different question from asking whether or not there is discrimination against individuals. To paraphrase the great Scottish philosopher David Hume, from the mere fact of differential statistical aggregates we can deduce no judgements about what those aggregates *should* be.

Furthermore, discriminating overtly against identifiable persons in order to achieve an acceptable overall pattern of distribution requires us to make the odious and arbitrary distinctions between persons that the rule against discrimination is designed to avoid and that the rule of law must seek to extirpate. The policy, to the extent that it purports to have a moral basis, is thus self-defeating.

Arbitrary distinctions between equal individuals are morally indefensible. This does not cease to be the case simply because the particular individuals whose interests are damaged happen to belong to some arbitrarily defined and contingent group like whites or men instead of some equally arbitrary category like blacks or women. The fact that the groups are defined by public policy rather than by private individuals may, in fact, make such policies more reprehensible than private discrimination.

As for the view that a good or desirable society is one in which there is an equal distribution of certain desired things across particular groups, this may be a perfectly reasonable view of the goals that a society might set itself. It is, however, a vision. It is based on values. Reasonable people, including democrats, can disagree about whether it is the right goal to pursue. There is no place for such a vision in a constitution that purports to set out the rules under which we may resolve the question of what goals we set ourselves at any given moment.

3) Finally, there are good reasons to doubt that greater substantive economic equality between individuals or groups is even realizable through the actions of government (including the courts). The good intentions of those who pursue this policy might always be frustrated, not least by the unintended consequences of their own policies.

If we accept the argument that statistical inequalities across groups are bad, and that the appropriate response is to replace private decisions with government orders (compulsory pay equity, hiring quotas, and so on), we enter a dangerous spiral in which the failure of relatively inoffensive policies becomes further evidence of ever more deeply entrenched discrimination, which justifies ever more government direction of our lives. The pursuit of group equality by government or the courts, then, must lead to a spiraling coercive and arbitrary interference in the private decisions of all individuals. The only way such interference could be justified is if it were necessary to protect us all from greater coercion (and hence interference in our free choices, as might be the case with conscription). This is the case neither for the majority nor for those supposedly in need of the help of reverse-discrimination policies to overcome institutional racism and sexism. Such policies thus represent a debatable social and political vision with which reasonable people can disagree without intellectual dishonesty and without being accused of merely defending their narrow self-interest. These do not belong in the Constitution.

To sum up, then, the 1982 Constitution introduces into the rules of the political game a great expansion of the previously limited vision and special status for identifiable groups that had been an element of the 1867 version. Having accepted this, we are now in a much weakened position to refuse distinct society or aboriginal self-government on principle or on high moral grounds. Such a refusal is to play favourites on values, something the liberal democratic account of legitimacy cannot digest in the long run. Once the principle is abandoned, we can, of course, discuss various values on their merits, but such discussions must always be inconclusive, with all that that implies for the legitimacy of what goes into the Constitution, as well as what stays out.

The lament for Leviathan is thus a lament for a whole way of thinking about constitutions and government that has gone out of fashion. It nevertheless represents the best hope for constitutional peace in the long run. Unfortunately, when we embarked on the road of constitutional visions, we unleashed a genie that is notoriously hard to recapture. Many people seem to believe these questions can be resolved by patient, rational argument about which visions are "justified" or "reasonable," but this fails to take the true measure of the non-rational attachment we all have to our particular visions.

It should be lamented as well, then, that we have allowed ourselves to be dragged onto this ground at all. Hobbes foresaw, rightly in my view, where this would lead. Once people's first political allegiance is to their private beliefs rather than to neutral political institutions that guarantee their safety from those who hold other beliefs, there is a long slow slide into anger, disunity, and disorder. It is possible to recover, but only when the atmosphere is so comprehensively soured that the "privatization" of vision becomes the only way out. Constitutions should eschew visions, but not because they are unimportant. On the contrary, visions are too important, too volatile, and too emotive to be contained successfully in such a frail vessel.

MEECH LAKE AND CHARLOTTETOWN ended their days as two more in a long list of failed constitutional reform proposals gathering dust in the National Archives. The matter does not, however, end there for many groups and interests. Let us focus on the one most likely, in the foreseeable future, to menace the future of Canada: Quebec.

Quebec's sense of grievance against the rest of the country has not been left where it was before the Quebec and Canada rounds began. If it were merely that expectations were raised that Quebec would get what it wanted, only to be dashed on the rocks of the sullen indifference of English-speaking Canada, we could probably survive that. What is vastly more important and incomparably more damaging is that these failures are understandably seen as a rejection by Canada of the importance of Quebec's current vision of itself when we were not willing to reject the visions of others in 1981–82. It is one thing to be told that your way of life will not be given constitutional recognition because no one's way of life is entitled to this; it is incomparably different to be told that others have arrogated to themselves the power to judge, and have found your way of life wanting while embracing others'.

To my mind three roads lie before us in dealing with our constitutional dilemmas. The first, which is embedded in our present Constitution quite independently of the changes proposed by Meech Lake and Charlottetown, is a future of constitutional bickering the scope of which cannot be foretold precisely. We can, nonetheless, measure its theoretical extent by trying to imagine what it would take to reconcile constitutional sanctions for all the possible self-definitions of Canadians now and in the future. Then add to that the dimension that some entrenched approvals will, as I've already suggested, obstruct the emergence of new self-definitions, and the vista of constitutional chopping and changing, tension and skirmishing that reveals itself becomes singularly unattractive.

The second road that beckons us is the one to take in an ideal world. We may not inhabit such a world, but sometimes the practices of other societies, even imaginary ones, help us to recognize our own imperfections, and help us to envision goals for which to aim. This route would take us back to square one, purging the Constitution of the substantive visions and values I've referred to. As a genuine framework for politics in a free society, it would refuse to use the coercive apparatus of the state to exalt and protect or to denigrate and obstruct ways of life that appear good to individual Canadians. I underline the renunciation of coercion because I believe that everything I have said so far is consistent with majorities using political institutions to make arguments for certain forms of life, as indeed they cannot avoid doing, for example, in the public schools. As Michael Oakeshott has said, one cannot avoid being educated in a tradition; at best one can choose the tradition in which one wishes to be educated. What is needed are constitutional guarantees against the government arrogating to itself a monopoly in schooling, the media, and so on, because it is such exclusive control that confers coercive power.

The utopianism of this view is perhaps enough to rule it out straight away. Political expediency alone probably makes it impossible, among other reasons, because it would involve depriving certain politically powerful groups of the recognition they won in earlier constitutional negotiations. Expediency is a poor counsellor, however, as such a purging of the Constitution would make the future of the country much more certain because it would break the destructive cycle of constitutional one-upmanship I have described. Certainly in practice many of these visions should be entrusted to the sure hands of benign neglect.

There may be other reasons for not following this road all the way to its logical destination — reasons of principle as well as of expediency — at the very least where Quebec is concerned, and perhaps more widely. Were one to follow through rigorously and consistently on the principles outlined so far, the Constitution of Canada would become a bulwark protecting individual Québécois from the heavy hand of a collectivist government, leaving them free to define themselves as anglophones, francophones, women, aboriginals or anything else one might care to imagine. To borrow a phrase from Rousseau, the collectively-minded franco-phones of *la belle province* would be "forced to be free"; the measures that this would justify would extend right up to military occupation to prevent Quebec from declaring itself independent. This strict logic would require that those residents of the national territory who refused to play willingly by the uniform national rules of behaviour either be forced to do so or asked to leave.

Yet the type of social order I have been praising in this essay cannot spring full-grown from the forehead of society, nor can it be imposed by constitutional fiat. It is, at bottom, a form of learned behaviour, an acquired self-constraint on the part of the bulk of society's members, that emerges slowly and painfully from gener-ations of trying to learn how people can best work together in the pursuit of the good life. The sort of realization I am describing, in which we all agree to put limits not just on how others will pursue their desires, but on how we will do so, dawns late on the human consciousness, and is at all times a fragile achievement. Kant was surely thinking of this when he said, "From the crooked timber of humanity, no straight thing was ever made." We must, in other words, do our best to create the conditions in which society will come to see the wisdom of such an approach to cooperation among people, many of whom will not share our vision of how the world could be made a better place.

One of the permanent features of human life is the evolution and change of individual identity. As society evolves, the pace and complexity of change accelerates dizzyingly. We cannot, then, be surprised if people seek stability in the eye of the storm. We want to be open to new senses of ourselves, to new ways of understand-ing our lives, but we want also to feel that we are true to who we are.

A deeply grounded historical identity like that of the Québécois can play the role of such a foundation for individual personality, which becomes all the more important when one can feel that foundation shifting under pressure from others who have other identities, rather than from internal pressures for new self-definition. Many Québécois have developed a psychology of *minoritaire* in which they have cast themselves as the victims of an insensitive English-speaking majority whose possession of some of the levers of political power is the prime obstacle to the proper development of the personality within Québécois culture. This view is not wholly without historical justification (although it has been vastly overdone), but that is not the thrust of my argument. My argument, rather, is that in such conditions too unnuanced an attempt to enforce the sort of neutral rules of social cooperation that I have described is bound to be perceived by the nationalist-minded as an ill disguised direct attempt at assimilation. In those circumstances, the value of the institutional guarantees of the free evolution of the individual personality might well be lost in the fears of assimilation, for the surest obstacle to one's full development is the sense that change is treason to one's people, to the group with which one's identity is currently intertwined.

It goes without saying, of course, that the Constitution does not exist in a vacuum, apart from ordinary politics. There are a thousand and one things that governments, both federal and provincial, as well as private individuals and groups, can and should do to overcome the weakening ties of interest and affection that bind individual Québécois to Canada. Such changes are perfectly necessary and legitimate as long as they do not seek to escape the civilizing control of the basic rules that should be the stuff of the Constitution.

We are progressively prevented from making such accommodations by a creeping suspicion that Canadian society and political institutions lack the necessary moral legitimacy in Quebec. My view, for what it is worth, is that this is the precise reverse of the truth: that the moral legitimacy of the national community is atrophying from lack of use. Pierre Bourgault, one of the most articulate founders of modern Quebec nationalism, once made a remark to the effect that when Canada believed in itself, perhaps the Québécois would as well. In short, I am optimistic about the ability and desire of ordinary Québécois to understand and abide by a liberal-individualist constitutionalism. Pessimism is, however, the order of the day when I see how willing national politicians are to undermine and even override these principles at the behest of self-seeking nationalist politicians from Quebec.

The second constitutional road thus has both a long-term and an immediate element. The long-term one is to know what is important and worth promoting and preserving in our constitutional tradition. That must guide us in the immediate task of muddling through in our relations with the Québécois, as we seek those thousand daily accommodations that make life bearable in a political community. Ironically, if I am right, compromising the principles of liberal democratic and individualist constitutionalism through the acceptance of tribalism will not preserve the country, but will make its demise more likely. Compromise has always been a great Canadian tradition, but there are some things on which one cannot, in conscience, compromise and some areas where compromise is destructive, not constructive. The trick is to know the difference.

The third road before us is one whose destination appears to me neither inevitable nor desirable, but which we must, nevertheless, confront directly. That is to prepare ourselves psychologically and politically to accept, if it comes to that, a desire by the Québécois to set for themselves a wholly made-in-Quebec set of rules of social cooperation; at its plainest, to cede them their sovereignty. There are all sorts of good and eminently practical reasons why this should be accompanied by a broad form of economic association, but I do not want to be distracted by this side issue. For the central concern is quite other: we must be prepared to recognize that it is a longing on the part of peoples everywhere to be *maîtres chez eux* and, that when faced with the choice, people have often preferred self-government to good government.

If this emotional reality is recognized, then we have to admit to ourselves that forcing Quebec to remain if the people of the province decide to go would be quite self-defeating. People cannot be protected from themselves, nor can they be forced to be tolerant, especially when the institutions doing the enforcing appear to be dominated by a majority whose growing numerical superiority is the cause of the malaise and insecurity of those in the minority.

One might even hope that, being deprived of a convenient and dependable scapegoat, the Québécois would be brought to confront the hard reality that victimization and oppression are always reciprocal relations, not one-way streets, and that being "in charge" means no more excuses. The old resignation of responsibility ("we are prevented from being what we might be by our malevolent oppressor") might give way to a new self-confidence, which is the cradle of tolerance and *ouverture sur le monde*. Might it even make clear, once and for all, the futility of political solutions to what are essentially problems of culture and individual identity?

Just as Bill 101 was a Trojan horse that forced the French-Canadians in Quebec to open themselves up to a whole new generation of French-speaking but ethnically diverse Québécois, independence would undoubtedly illustrate magisterially that we cannot ground our individual identity or protect ourselves from personal insecurities by any mere constitutional form, or by forcing people by law to adopt a particular form of life. As author and explorer of the human spirit Laurens van der Post put it, "The only way an identity or spirit can survive is on its merit to life."

The Vindication of Doubt

MANY READERS, BOTH hostile and friendly, have asked me about the general ideas underlying these essays. The ideas are hard to place in the traditional categories of Left or Right. My essays are hostile to collectivism of a certain kind and celebrate individualism as one of the great achievements of Western civilization. For many this puts me on the Right, although how they square that with my dislike of established authority or my egalitarianism or my vaguely anarchist leanings remains a mystery to me.

On the other hand, I have no time for the cultural conservatives who believe, with Plato, that they understand the one right way to live, which is universal and immutable. I am a utilitarian and a bit of a skeptic: I believe that we will never stop discovering new aspects of ourselves and the world, and, therefore, that our conception of the good life must always be changing. Natural hierarchy or unearned privilege are repugnant to me. All of this gives me strong affinities to the Left.

But there is no need to resolve the question of which camp I belong in, for it is precisely one of my goals to resist easy classification under the shallow categories of pundits and journalists. Pigeonholing often announces the closing of the mind. Instead, I propose to offer the reader some brief insight into one of the most important influences on my own thought: F. A. Hayek, Nobel Prize–winning economist and social philosopher, and midwife at the rebirth of classical liberalism in twentieth-century Europe.

My first book was to be the definitive debunking of Hayek, who I then believed was a dangerous political thinker. But like Tom Sawyer's young friends, though I came to jeer, I stayed to paint.

While remaining a stranger to many of Hayek's commitments, my whole way of thinking about life, society, and politics has been transformed by meeting this remarkable man. In 1990, CBC Radio's *Ideas* carried a two-part series on Hayek, which I wrote and narrated. This is a revised version of the transcript, presented here in essay form. At the end, I have listed the people I interviewed for the programs, whose ideas have now been incorporated in the essay.

THE MARKET IS THE CENTRAL FEATURE of Freiburg, a town in southwest Germany near the source of the Danube River. The market occupies the entire square surrounding the medieval red sandstone cathedral, and it is to this crossroads of the region that farmers and shoppers have been drawn every week for centuries.

Picture the scene: frugal housewives move from table to table, comparing prices of fruits, vegetables, sausages, and flowers. In their stalls, beefy, red-faced farmers fuss with their awnings to protect their wares from the overhead sun. It's been a hot, dry month across much of Europe, but the skeptical housewives are unimpressed as the farmers blame the weather for driving up the price of local tomatoes. Freiburg market has existed here for centuries. This scene has been repeated a thousand times. Its very banality might lead us to take it for granted, to fail to wonder at the order that underlies this anarchy of individual negotiations and transactions. But order there is, one that includes the industrial system that provides the tractors, ploughs, and fertilizers used to produce the food. It includes the farmers' judgements about what to plant, and how, and when. The transportation system is part of this order. And so are the customers themselves, with their incomes from countless other activities.

Until his death in March 1992, there lived within the sound of

Brian Lee Crowley

those Freiburg cathedral bells a man who saw in marketplaces such as this one a much broader order, an order that touches us through language and law, and morality. From the functioning of markets, Friedrich Hayek drew the insights for a social philosophy that he himself described as both radical and reactionary. In the 1970s, his thought fostered the rise of the New Right. In the early 1990s, many of the new democratic regimes of Eastern Europe relied on his inspiration to direct their economies away from communism.

In 1974, Hayek, a tall, austere figure, rose in Stockholm's Palace of Concerts to receive a Nobel Prize in Economics. At the time many countries, including Canada, were beginning to face the problem of simultaneous inflation and unemployment. It was a bewildering one-two punch that their economists couldn't explain — but one that Hayek had predicted many years earlier. Now, recognition for this work was at hand. Hayek used the occasion to make a characteristically frank assessment of the discipline of economics, an assessment that tells us a great deal about Hayek's deeply held beliefs.

As a profession, we have made a mess of things. It seems to me that this failure of economics to guide policy more successfully is closely connected with our general propensity to imitate as closely as possible the procedures of the brilliantly successful physical sciences, an attempt which in our field may lead to serious error. It is an approach which has come to be described as the "Scientistic" attitude; an attitude, as I defined it some thirty years ago, which is decidedly unscientific in the true sense of the word, since it involves a mechanical and uncritical application of thought to fields different from those in which they have been originally formed. If man is not to do more harm than good in his efforts to improve the social order he will have to learn that in this, as in all other fields where essential complexity of an organized kind prevails, he cannot acquire that full knowledge which would make mastery of the events possible.

The Nobel Prize marked Hayek's return to professional respectability. Early on, he had set himself against the hubris of theoreticians who proposed through science to reshape society to some ideal form. His stand was unwelcome among intellectuals, but it was deeply grounded both in his experience and in his reflections on the tumultuous events through which he had lived.

Hayek's story begins in Vienna, only a few hundred miles downstream on the Danube from his home in Freiburg. He was born in 1899, a child of the professional middle class. His father was a doctor, later a lecturer in biology at the University of Vienna. In this twilight era before the first World War, Vienna ranked with Paris, Berlin, and London among the capitals of Europe. The House of Hapsburg ruled from the city over an empire of fifty million people that stretched from the Alps to the Balkan states.

One has only to think of all the names associated with Vienna during Hayek's own early life to realize how glorious was the Vienna of pre-1914: Sigmund Freud in psychoanalysis, Ludwig Wittgenstein (a distant cousin of Hayek's) in philosophy, Gustav Klimt and the foundations of Art Nouveau, Hans Kelsen in legal theory, Anton Bruckner, Gustav Mahler, Arnold Schoenberg in music. For some reason, many of the great modern schools of study began in Vienna: psychology, economics, philosophy. The best and brightest from all around Central Europe were drawn to Vienna. To newcomers with ambition and ideas, the Viennese offered a discerning and sophisticated hearing. In Vienna, as perhaps nowhere else, people were ready to debate ideas, to reject some, advance others, explore all. Hayek would later recall this intellectual climate as an essential quality of the city of his birth.

Underlying the rich brilliance of the Vienna into which Hayek was born was the traditional order of the Hapsburg Empire. It was not a very democratic or egalitarian order, but it provided an essential framework of law, tradition, and custom, within which economic, social, and intellectual life could flourish. On the gateway of the Imperial Palace, a Latin inscription faced the emperor's windows: *Iustitia Regnorum Fundamentum* (Justice is the Basis of Your Reign). The empire assured formal equality before the law to all members of its many cultural and ethnic groups. In return, it demanded of all citizens that they place respect for the law ahead of group loyalties. To supporters of the empire, the supremacy of the law was beyond question. But not to others. Opposed to the imperial ideal was the growing nationalism of Czechs, Slovaks, Romanians, Galacians, and Serbs. To the middle classes of Vienna, the passion of nationalism was the enemy of all that they valued.

In 1914, the nationalist challenge to the empire ignited the Great War that changed the map of Europe. Four years later the empire was in ruins, and the glory of Vienna was shattered. Hayek joined in the fighting when he was seventeen; he served in an artillery battalion on the Italian front. The Vienna to which he returned in November 1918 was a city transformed: with the empire dismembered, the city was now the capital of a little Austrian rump, and new forces were shaping its social and political life. In the City of Vienna, for example, there was a powerful socialist administration that broke new ground in creating programs to favour working-class housing and new forms of urban living. All of this required heavy subsidization, which was financed by a growing tax burden on the bourgeoisie. The old order of comfort and privilege for the few was under vigorous attack.

A young man, just returned from the front and about to enter university, Hayek was at first sympathetic to the emerging new order. Like most young intellectuals of the day, he was attracted by the new promise of socialism and described himself at this time as a sort of Fabian, referring to a group of intellectuals influential in the founding of the British Labour Party. His mild socialism drew him to the study of economics, which he saw as revealing the methods of solving much of the misery of the human condition.

This attraction to socialism, however, had to coexist with the destruction of a society and way of life that also had their claims on Hayek's allegiance. The devastation of the old order was reaching its climax just as Hayek was leaving university. Inflation was raging through the economies of Central Europe. Paper money became virtually worthless. Carefully built-up savings were lost overnight. For the young economist it was an indelible experience. He often told the story of how proud he was when, in the fall of 1921, he got his first job. His salary of five thousand Austrian kronen per month seemed to him princely, because he remembered that just a few short years before his father's salary for the entire year had also been five thousand kronen. Within ten months of taking this job, Hayek's salary had risen to one million kronen. The very fabric of society was unraveling.

At this point, Hayek encountered a man who was to have a decisive influence on his development: Ludwig von Mises. Mises was a singular figure in Vienna, a short square man with a large moustache and a closely cropped head of white hair. He was a brilliant but disagreeable economist, not a university professor, but a civil servant — the senior administrator of the Chamber of Commerce in Vienna. From his office he ran a private seminar in economics, and it was here that Hayek, as he said later, was cured of his early socialism. Mises was of the Austrian school of economics, a body of thought that emphasized the role of human knowledge in the creation of wealth. When Hayek first joined him, Mises had just published a book that dealt with the question: "Is socialism an economic possibility?" It was a raging issue in a world still stunned by the Russian Revolution, and in a Vienna dominated by a Marxist-inspired socialist party.

In the 1920s there was, of course, a tremendous debate concerning the feasibility of a socialist economy, because there had never been such a thing. At that time socialism as an alternative to capitalism was basically seen as a utopia. In the debate on the feasibility of socialism Mises took the position that it was simply impossible, because without a market and without the price signals that arise from a market it was impossible to allocate resources between alternative uses. In socialist economies, he argued, planners would try to balance supply and demand by calculating how many shoes and cars and houses people will need, and then ordering that amount to be made. But the planners will never get it right, Mises insisted. He said it will be a practical impossibility for them to gather all the knowledge they will require about either people's needs and desires, or the means and resources available to satisfy them. The reason is that such knowledge is spread among too many people. Each of us as consumers and workers or employers possess part of this knowledge, but only part. Where the market succeeds, and the planners fail, is in tapping into this knowledge and putting it to effective use.

Through the operation of the market, for example, the shoemaker learns quickly and clearly which styles or models he should produce; people will tell him, through the price they're willing to pay, or not pay, for any particular kind of shoe. In this sense, the price is a signal, and prices, said Mises, are a form of communication. Hayek would call this the fundamental concept of economics:

> Prices act as guides telling you what you ought to do. It's only because we orient ourselves at market prices that we are informed in what way we can best contribute to the needs of society. Prices are not really determined by what people have done, as classical economics and particularly Marxist economics still believe. It's not the labour which determines value; it's the value which determines how much labour we ought to put into a thing and even more important not how much labour we ought to put into it but into what we ought to put our labour. And that we can only know because in a modern large society we're all working to satisfy needs of people we don't even know. We are part of a system which nobody can survey in a comprehensive manner, and that it is an orderly system is entirely due to that steering mechanism of the market. In an open market prices tell us where best to put in our efforts, and the functioning of this system depends essentially on free, uncontrolled prices.

In the 1920s, the socialist experiments of our century were barely under way, their outcomes still unknown. The problems of capitalism, however, were about to become devastatingly apparent. The traumatic stock market crash of October 1929 revealed a stunning loss of confidence in the economy. The Great Depression of the 1930s drained faith in the entire system. Bankruptcies, unemployment, and poverty reached levels that challenged all conventional assumptions about economic management. Political extremism intensified. In the radical analysis of both right and left, free-market capitalism had had its day; it was now in its death throes. Throughout the industrialized world — in Britain, America, Germany, France — appeals went up to replace the invisible hand of a failed market system with the strong arm of political authority.

Hayek's initial attempt to sketch out his understanding of the dynamics of capitalism was contained in an influential book, *Prices and Production*, published in 1931. By now his reputation as a rigorous and productive theoretical economist of the free-market persuasion had spread abroad. In Britain it reached the ears of Lionel Robbins, head of the Economics Department of the London School of Economics. The Depression had hit Britain hard. Unemployment was measured in the millions. The Labour Party, anathema to the establishment, had become a force to be reckoned with. At this time, even more than today, the City of London was a pinnacle of world finance. London financiers were unsettled by what appeared to them as the radicalism of new economic theories gaining ground in the universities, particularly at Cambridge, under the guidance of John Maynard Keynes. Robbins, a patrician free-market economist well connected in London, was looking for someone to do battle with Keynes. He found his man in the young Austrian economist.

In the fiscally conservative circles of London, Keynes's economic ideas were seen as particularly worrisome. As someone who had established a brilliant reputation as the expositor of free-market economics, Hayek seemed the perfect counterfoil to the more dirigiste ideas of Keynes, which were considered in some circles to border on the subversive.

Brian Lee Crowley

Hayek had met Keynes in 1928 and, although disagreeing with him on economics, had formed a friendship with him. Now the two were to become scholarly opponents in a controversy that would continue even after Keynes's death in 1946. John Maynard Keynes was not merely an economist with an imposing reputation. He was one of the most remarkable personalities of this century, as his former students and colleagues all testified. He was a man of genius, a Renaissance man to whom everything came easily. When he spoke, he cast a kind of spell over his listeners, and he left a deep impression on all who knew him. Hayek was no exception. Those who knew Hayek at this time say that he was a little mesmerized by Keynes, by his effortless ability with anything mathematical, with economics, with art, with money. By contrast, Hayek was a dour man, stiffly bourgeois, who took everything he did with a deadly seriousness. It was not for him to easily toss off solutions to complex problems. He wanted and needed to take the time and trouble to think things through carefully for himself. Hayek thought Keynes too talented by half.

One incident summed up for Hayek all the distrust and misgivings he felt towards Keynes (and incidentally illustrated Hayek's own earnest pedestrian approach to his work). Soon after his arrival in England, Hayek spent the better part of a year carefully reading, analysing, and then criticizing Keynes's most recent book on economics. He published a thorough and exhaustive critical review, only to be told by Keynes that he shouldn't have wasted his time, for he (Keynes) himself no longer believed in the book's ideas.

Hayek's misgivings about Keynes and his circle — mostly the famous Bloomsbury group of intellectuals — soon went far beyond mere technical disagreements about dry controversies in economics. He rapidly came to the view that these influential thinkers and writers recognized no limits to what human intelligence could do. Their view seemed to be that the human mind was up to discovering the workings of every aspect of life, and by taking

150

thought, improving on them. The twentieth century seemed to them the age of great enlightenment; it would sweep away old traditions, customs and habits that stood in the way of human happiness. In economics, this meant that one should abandon the old notions of self-correcting markets that work slowly, and only in the long run. The market, left to itself, had produced the human suffering and waste of the Depression. Surely brilliant minds could use the science of economics to do better.

Keynes had, of course, written about money and cycles before, but in 1936 he came to write about a fundamental doubt that unregulated markets can always lead to full employment. He tried to establish the idea that markets, without any outside interference, could get stuck in a situation where you have less than full employment. In the midst of scarcity you would have a waste of resources, and Keynes's view was that unless some external help came, the economy would not get out of this trap.

The external help that Keynes was proposing was to increase the purchasing power of consumers — put more money into their pockets. If the economy was in a trap of permanently high unemployment, he argued, use the tools that government has at its disposal to increase demand. The means he proposed for doing so are by now familiar. Extra demand was to be created, Keynes said, by manipulating interest rates, cutting taxes, and spending on public works such as roads, sewers, and so forth. The stimulus to the economy would create new jobs, unemployment would fall; we would spend our way out of the slump. True, the economy might not be able to keep up with all the new spending power of consumers. Some of the new money might just go into higher prices. Keynes acknowledged this threat of inflation, but he was confident that it could be contained through clever management.

Keynes presented his recommendations in a General Theory in 1936. Hayek was not persuaded. No doubt Keynes's approach would create jobs in the short run, but Hayek could not forget the lesson of inflation in the early 1920s. Keynes's plan to inflate the economy would distort the signaling mechanism of prices and incomes. False signals would lead people into jobs that existed only because of government action. Hayek foresaw the creation of a true vicious circle in which larger amounts of inflationary spending would be required to maintain employment. At first, though, he chose not to respond to Keynes's General Theory. He thought it might be yet another of the brilliant prescriptions that Keynes tossed off and then discarded. This time he was mistaken. The world was desperate for answers to the Depression, and Keynes's promise of full employment met with an eager response, first in the universities, then in governments, as the new economic policy-makers spread the word.

Hayek knew that Keynes had triumphed, and the pill must have been a bitter one to swallow. He'd been brought from Austria explicitly to be the champion of free-market thinking and had been bested by Keynes, whose interventionist theories would become a new orthodoxy. Far from making his reputation — and that had been on his mind when he came to London — he was forgotten by those who earlier had listened to him with attention.

But Hayek was to have his day, even though it would take thirty years. He was always clear that Keynes's grand schemes would reduce unemployment, but in such a way as to damage the economy in the long run, for precisely the reasons that he and Mises had opposed central planning: by causing inflation, central planning wreaked havoc with the signaling mechanism of prices. There resulted a long-term misallocation of resources as people followed the price signals into jobs that existed solely because inflation had distorted those signals. In the long run, this was to bring in its train an imbalance between productive investment and consumption. The name we gave to this phenomenon of simultaneous inflation and unemployment in the 1970s was stagflation. Hayek had foreseen this result in his 1931 book *Production and Prices*, and the 1970s was Hayek's decade *because* he had foreseen, forty years before the fact, what the consequences of Keynesian policies would be. The importance of what he had done could not be recognized until the conditions he had theorized about became real. In the late 1930s all this was in the future. The direction of Hayek's career seemed firmly established. He was a family man, a respected, if somewhat stuffy, professor at the London School of Economics, and arch-defender of free-market orthodoxy. The socialist Beatrice Webb described him as a man who thinks, talks, and writes abstract economics. In fact, he was a man profoundly at odds with his profession. It was not just that he opposed the growing support for economic planning and government intervention; he questioned the very direction in which the study of economics was headed. A dangerous confusion had overtaken the field, he believed, a misunderstanding about the nature and the limits of science. In some cases, he was prepared to concede, the mistake was innocent, a misguided attempt to apply the techniques of the natural sciences to the problems of unemployment and poverty. Other cases were more ominous: the so-called scientific socialism of Marxism in the Soviet Union, and the pseudoscientific racial theories of the Nazi movement. But in all cases Hayek saw a common thread: a belief in a grand theoretical view of a better world, and an unlimited faith in the ability of our reason to engineer human society.

Hayek understood the enormous appeal of science. World War II was the age of the boffins, the scientific wizards who brought their knowledge to the service of the state. Their creations — the computer, revolutionary advances in aeronautics and electronics, the atomic bomb — all would testify to the power of the scientific method. Why not apply the same scientific principles to the orga-nization of human society?

Economic planners proposed to do just this: use their knowledge to manipulate the economy in order to produce better results than undirected market forces permit. Comprehensive overall planning was passé; all economists needed to do was manipulate a few key factors — inflate the money supply or control rents or interests rates, for example. Such manipulation was precisely the approach that had produced the scientific marvels on which our everyday activities depend. At the push of a button we can beam television images around the world or send missiles hurtling into outer space. Why should we be unable to find the economic button that eliminates unemployment, or the social button that reduces poverty?

The simple answer is that a human organization, or society, is not a mechanical system. You can control to some extent mechanical orders that you invent. A motor can be controlled and engineered and designed. But a human order consists of individuals with differing ends and purposes. The knowledge they deal with is decentralized across an enormous number of individuals.

To a determined scientific mind, of course, the complexity of human society might just be an added challenge. Yes, human knowledge is spread broadly across society and is difficult for anyone to comprehend entirely. But if the only problem is the vast quantity of information, then the solution may simply be to enlarge the effort. Hire more people to ask more questions. Hayek rejected this reasoning. Human behaviour, he insisted, cannot be predicted reliably on the basis of the past. How we react to any given event depends on what we know at the time, and what we know is constantly changing.

Later, critics would accuse Hayek of being anti-intellectual. In fact, he had reached the view that by its nature human knowledge is elusive. A truth known through the centuries is that we are often unable to put the most important things into words. A favourite illustration is a parable by the Chinese scholar Chuang-Tzu.

A wheelwright asks a nobleman what book he's reading; when told it is the collected wisdom of dead sages, the workman dismisses it as without value. The nobleman threatens the man with death unless he can justify his impudence. The wheelwright replies, "Speaking as a wheelwright, I look at it this way. When I'm making a wheel, if my stroke is too slow, then it bites deep, but is not steady.

If my stroke is too fast, then it is steady but does not go deep. The right pace, neither slow nor fast, cannot get into the hand unless it comes from the heart. It is a thing that cannot be put into words or rules. There is an art in it that I cannot explain to my son. That is why I cannot let him take over my work, and here I am at seventy, still making wheels. In my opinion, it must have been the same with the men of old. All that was worth handing on died with them. The rest they put in their books."

Such tacit knowledge underlies much of any society's creativity and productivity. Yet it resists rational inquiry, said Hayek, and poses grave questions about our ability to understand in a theoretical sense the world we inhabit.

This isn't as startling as it might sound. There is a philosophical tradition that is skeptical, that doubts that we can have complete knowledge of any system, any order of events. This philosophical tradition (which David Hume's thought exemplifies) says that there are two sorts of knowledge in the world. There is knowledge that you can reproduce — mathematical knowledge, knowledge of physical systems. But a social system is characterized by a second sort of knowledge: that of time and place, knowledge you can't express in words, intuitive knowledge.

Hayek, then, spent a good deal of his war years working out his opposition to Keynes's arguments, and the consequences of following Keynesian policies: accelerating inflation, with the havoc it would wreak on the function of prices, in a competitive market place, to gather and disseminate information. From there it was only a short step to a far more disturbing insight. If such policies are pursued, then the intervention of the government in the economy will grow inexorably, as the discoordination between economic activities it introduces becomes more and more apparent and the appearance of order can only be restored by central direction. But before 1944 Hayek was almost solely concerned with the technical economics of the question, and had not yet accepted that a direct appeal to public opinion was necessary.

By the end of the war his view had changed. Public opinion in the West, deeply influenced by the success of the war effort in its comprehensive government direction of all social activity, was moving strongly in favour of peacetime planning. The British Labour party swept to a stunning victory in 1945 on the slogan "And now win the peace," suggesting that the methods appropriate to winning the war were also appropriate to peacetime.

Sensing what was coming, in 1944 Hayek went on the offensive. He published *The Road to Serfdom*. This uncharacteristically polemical tract made his name almost a household word after the war, and earned him the undying enmity of the Left. The book warned that economic planning as a way to end unemployment and poverty would have consequences far beyond anyone's intentions. As stronger and stronger government intervention was required to maintain stability in the absence of the coordinating signals of prices, economic freedom would gradually be extinguished. Political freedom could not be far behind.

It would be hard to imagine a position more out of step with the mood of the day. In 1942, a Royal Commission under Sir William Beveridge had captivated public opinion in Britain with recommendations for a national insurance scheme including free health care for all. Coming so soon after Beveridge, *The Road to Serfdom* touched off a firestorm of controversy, as Hayek himself recognized:

> I usually hear it said that I became famous by that book. But the fact is I made myself frightfully unpopular with that book. That was the real effect. I had been, I think, quite a respected economic theorist, and then I came out with a great attack on all economic planning and socialism, just at a time when good people had just discovered the great attractions of socialism. By becoming a popular author — it sold well, I can't deny, much beyond any of my expectations — in professional circles my reputation sank to zero, and I had to work for a very long time to regain my reputation.

In England, some intellectuals on the Left were open to at least part of Hayek's argument. George Orwell remarked: "In the negative part of Professor Hayek's thesis there is a great deal of truth. It cannot be said too often that collectivism is not inherently democratic, but on the contrary gives to a tyrannical minority such powers as the Spanish Inquisition never dreamt of." Orwell's reaction was, however, exceptional, as Hayek's work was vilified almost everywhere, especially in the United States.

Before so much incomprehension and hostility, it might have been understandable had Hayek decided that the political game wasn't worth the candle and returned to his technical economics. Instead it only seemed to whet his appetite for controversy and make him realize that if he was serious in his belief that sound political and economic ideas made a sound social order possible, then his intellectual tasks were only just beginning.

Clearly, though, the direct populist course he had tried with *The Road to Serfdom* did not suit the needs of his personality nor the complexity of his message. So he embarked on the postwar period with two objectives in mind: to flesh out the political and economic message that underlay his liberal economics, and to create an international network of intellectuals committed to those ideas.

He had no illusions about the difficulties that lay before him. The reaction among intellectuals to *The Road to Serfdom*, perhaps more than any other single incident, made Hayek reflect that it was not enough to appeal to intellectuals with ideas. Intellectuals, he came to believe, were mesmerized by the prospect of social control — and even wholesale social engineering — that appeared to be the direction of postwar evolution. The fascination with power had taken hold of them, for the power that was to be given to public authorities to plan and intervene was to be exercised predominantly by intellectuals. Hayek took it as his special project to prick the balloon of their illusion that this social planning would be guided by scientific rationality and objective technical expertise. The rage of which he became the object seemed to him to be explicable only by understanding that he had called into question the pride and presumption of the very people whose support he sought.

It was this unwavering doubt that seemed to be vindicated many years later, not only by the Nobel Prize, but by the failure of communism and the fall of the Berlin Wall. The most advanced and technologically sophisticated attempt to reinvent human society along rationally planned lines had collapsed under the weight of its own contradictions. Thirty years after the appearance of *The Road to Serfdom* in his Nobel Prize acceptance speech, Hayek characteristically appealed yet again to social scientists and intellectuals not to allow scientific progress to blind them to the very real limits of human ability:

> There is danger in the exuberant feeling of ever-growing power which the advance of the physical sciences has engendered, and which tempts man to try, dizzy with success, to use a famous phrase of the early period of communism, to subject not only our natural, but also our human environment to the control of human will. The recognition of the insuperable limits to his knowledge ought indeed to teach the student of society a lesson of humility which should guard him from becoming an accomplice in man's fatal striving to control society; a striving that makes him not only a tyrant over his fellows, but which may well make him the destroyer of a civilization which no brain has designed, but which has grown from the efforts of millions of individuals.

Keynes at least had appreciated Hayek's misgivings about government intervention. The new postwar breed of economists in government and the universities had little such respect. To them, Hayek represented the failure of classical economics. Even during the depths of the Depression he had argued that there was little the government could or should do in the short run to create jobs. He had clung to the idea that the best policy was to establish conditions that would let the economy recover in the long run. The Keynesians were set against such "do-nothing" economics. In turn, Hayek regarded them as perpetrators of what he called "scientism": a belief that the techniques we use to manipulate the natural world can be transferred to the management of the human world. Hayek was extremely depressed about the way the intellectual world was going, as well as the way the economic world was going. He'd always held the view that ideas are decisive in the determination of social events. That's a view, of course, that Keynes held; it's perhaps the only view they had in common. Hayek believed that the postwar errors in economic management would not be repeated, but would be altered or even corrected under the right intellectual atmosphere. Of course, in the 1950s and 1960s the opposite intellectual atmosphere, at least from Hayek's point of view, was being created. The economic system seemed to be working rather well, and prosperity under Keynesian methods had been achieved. What Hayek feared was that people would not understand the consequences of such measures. And if the intellectual world had virtually abandoned the sort of theories he grew up with, they wouldn't have an explanation of how to put things right when the Keynesian system inevitably failed.

Hayek's fears extended beyond Britain. Across Europe, communists had put up disciplined active resistance to the Nazis during the war. Now they were filling the political vacuum left by the fall of the Third Reich. In Western Europe, communist parties were a force to be reckoned with. In Eastern Europe they were taking over. In Czechoslovakia, for example, elections in 1948 gave the communists a parliamentary majority, and mass demonstrations by workers in Prague soon gave them control of the government. The Iron Curtain, as Churchill had just called it, was about to divide Europe. Hayek feared that the death of economic freedom in the East might be a forerunner of what lay ahead for the West. He believed it essential to counter the move to government intervention before it undermined Western economies.

Hayek's most important contribution here was in founding a

network of intellectuals to disseminate liberal and free-market ideas. He explicitly wished to found a group to rival the well-organized networks of intellectuals on the Left who worked so tirelessly to discredit the ideas of the liberal social and economic order. In 1947 Hayek brought together thirty-six academics, economists, historians, and journalists to create the Mount Pelerin Society. The name was taken from the mountain near Lake Geneva in Switzerland where the first meeting of the group was held. The Society rapidly grew from three dozen members to well over five hundred.

The guests at the first Mont Pelerin conference were recruits in a new ideological crusade, and they would prove to be able warriors. Among the Americans present was Milton Friedman, the flamboyant monetary theorist from the University of Chicago who later would also win a Nobel Prize. Hayek was about to become a colleague of Friedman's. In 1950 he joined the University of Chicago — not as an economist, however, but as a professor of social and moral sciences. The next ten years were to be among the most creative of Hayek's life. He would use them to sharpen, deepen, and refine the social and political ideas that support the economic order. And from the rich intellectual heritage of Western Europe and the United States, he would assemble his argument that much of human progress itself springs from economic liberty:

> There are now about two hundred times as many people living on this earth than were living here five thousand years ago. It was not anything which man intellectually designed. It was not mainly, as is commonly believed, the advance of science or technology which taught us new methods. It is solely the result of most of humanity having for the last few thousand years adopted a moral tradition which included private property, which was the basis of the market, the basis of the exchange, the basis of all kinds of practical rules of conduct which enabled us unwittingly to build an overall order of mankind.

The essential feature of any economy, beyond the village level, is the exchange of goods or services among people who may be complete strangers to each other. We serve people we do not know, says Hayek, and are served by others equally ignorant of our existence. This ignorance is inescapable. Moreover, as the economic system develops, it becomes ever greater. The more people involved in the system, the more different skills that are required, the more impossible it becomes for any one person to know everything there is to know. This is why central planning of the economy must fail, Hayek said. No government agency could possess all the information it would need to replace the market. And our ignorance of economic knowledge, he argued, is but one example of our inability to understand either ourselves or the world in which we live.

What Hayek found even more remarkable than our ignorance, however, is the way in which the economy makes use of the knowledge and skills each of us possesses. In a market economy, he observed, the price system coordinates and directs our activity. If the price of beef goes up, for example, I may switch to chicken, and the beef farmer may decide it is worthwhile to raise more cattle for sale. No one has to tell either of us what to do; we both respond spontaneously to the same price signal. The economy, said Hayek, consists of millions of such independent actions. The order we may see in it is not the result of any overall plan, but the unintended product of spontaneous activity by individuals and firms. It is a spontaneous order.

To grasp this principle of a market order as an extended order arising spontaneously without conscious human direction, we need only cast our minds back to the emergence of trade in the earliest times. Archaeologists are constantly bringing to light further evidence of an intricate network of trade relations between widely dispersed primitive peoples. Wishing only to satisfy their own desires, these peoples were driven to trade goods they had in abundance for rarer commodities from exotic places: British tin for Mediterranean wines, North African grain for Middle Eastern cloth, and so forth. This constant quest for new trading possibilities created new contacts and cross-fertilization, the fruits of which could never have been imagined or planned. Who would have guessed, for example, that Marco Polo's voyages to the Orient would bring back noodles on which the Italians would build an entire pasta-based cuisine? Or that he would bring back gunpowder, changing European military strategy forever by making fortresses and armour obsolete?

Hayek would not say that all our economic activity occurs without planning. On the contrary, intensive planning is very much a characteristic of modern industry. The economy may be a spontaneous order, but it is by no means an anarchy. He uses a word that he borrowed from the Greeks; this kind of order is what he calls a catallaxy — a collection of innumerable little planning organizations. A firm is like a little economy; it knows it must meet a certain contractual commitment — it must produce shoes at a certain price. It must satisfy a demand for those shoes, or else it goes out of business. That is a planning organization. Anybody who's worked in any kind of organization knows that targets have to be met. Targets are met in small organizations by using knowledge of other organizations because they're setting prices and standards for competition. All these little economies compete with each other, or more precisely, cooperate with each other, in a competitive environment that Hayek would call a catallaxy — an overall order, which is not an organization, not planned. What is planned are all the actions of the individuals and corporations within that overall catallaxy.

This spontaneous economic order — where millions of firms and individuals plan and cooperate and compete with each other — does not fit easily into either of the two worlds into which we normally divide our experience. Traditionally thinkers have distinguished between the natural world, not created by us, and a world that is artificial, one that we have invented and can control.

Hayek defines a third category: a world consisting of myriad human institutions that are, to use one of his favourite phrases, "the product of human action but not of human design":

> The confusion in this field is largely due to the dichotomy which derives from the ancient Greeks, between the natural and the artificial. There is, between the natural and the artificial, the cultural which is neither natural nor artificial, but is the outcome of a process of selection which was not a deliberate one, but is due to the fact that certain ways of behaving have proved more successful than others, without anybody understanding why they were more successful. Now that of course is neither natural nor artificial; I think the only word we have for it is cultural. Culture is not artificial, because culture has never been designed by anybody. It is not a human invention. In fact I would go so far as to say that it is not the mind which has produced culture, but culture which has produced the mind.

Hayek's interest in this zone between the natural and the artificial led to some of his most challenging and controversial insights. Human culture, he said, is expressed through many artifacts. A simple handsaw, for example, is the product of knowledge about how to make and temper steel, how to roll it into sheets, how to cut the teeth and at what angles. When you think about it, the saw represents a considerable body of knowledge that has been developed and refined over many years. But, Hayek says, cultural knowledge is also expressed through our institutions — our sports and religions and moral and ethical systems. These, too, have developed over time, and their complexity suggests that they also have emerged not from a single plan or design, but through the same spontaneous processes as the market.

Hayek was attracted to law as a particularly significant example of a spontaneous order, and as an essential condition for economic freedom. Law regulates and limits our economic behaviour, but it also provides the predictability that enables us to plan. The law ensures that we cannot be deprived of the reward for our efforts. Through the law we can define what is ours and what we may protect from others.

The central role Hayek gives to law in his vision of a self-regulating society has made him the object of considerable criticism on the grounds that his supposedly "spontaneous" order is, in fact, merely the product of laws, which are human institutions invented by very human lawmakers. But Hayek argues that this completely misunderstands the role of lawgivers, particularly in the common-law tradition, but more generally in legal orders that base themselves on observed human behaviour. In such an order, lawmakers do not pick the rules of law out of a vacuum or some ideologue's vision of the ideal world; on the contrary, they try to tease out of the regularities of people's behaviour a description of those regularities. Lawmakers identify those behaviours that are important enough that rulers, police officers, and judges ought to ensure they are followed.

One graphic example of how people following their own ends can nevertheless produce orderly patterns of behaviour can be found by comparing two colleges in the American Midwest. Each college completed an extension at the same time. In one, the landscaping was completed immediately, including beautifully laid-out paths and walkways. In the other, the landscaping was left unfinished for a year to allow the students the time to establish the pathways they found most useful to them. At the end of one year, the most heavily traveled areas were paved over, creating a system of pathways that met the students' needs precisely. In the college that had planned its paths abstractly for their aesthetic beauty rather than their usefulness, the picture was rather different. There, ugly pathways were worn in the carefully laid-out lawns as the students found shortcuts to their destinations, shortcuts that did not fit in the planners' grand schemes.

In 1960, Hayek published his initial defence of spontaneous order in *The Constitution of Liberty*. The book met with general indifference. Once again, as at the time of *The Road to Serfdom*, public opinion was headed in a far different direction. The United States had been in recession in the late 1950s and now a new president, John F. Kennedy, was promising to get the economy moving again. The spirit of Keynes was apparent in some of his policies, and as the decade went on they would get the credit for an unprecedented economic expansion. Kennedy personified a new confidence among Americans in the ability of government to intervene successfully in the development of society, a confidence that *The Constitution of Liberty* declared was misplaced. Being out of step with the times, however, was nothing new to Hayek. In 1962 he returned to teach in Europe, and there set out to develop his thoughts in a massive three-volume book that appeared in the following decade. Entitled *Law, Legislation and Liberty*, the work was not just a comprehensive statement of Hayek's ideas. Not only did legal, economic, and moral cultures evolve over time, Hayek now argued, but the competition between different cultural and social traditions meant that some would flourish, and others would languish. Through a process of evolutionary selection, those cultural practices that confer success on those who observe them will proliferate. Success, as the saying goes, breeds success. Implicit in this argument is the idea that some cultural practices are better suited than others to survive. But Hayek carefully distinguished his concept from biological evolution.

> While biological inheritance rests on the selection of individuals, and at present it is even the fashion among biologists to deny that there is such a thing as group selection, my point will be that cultural selection is essentially a phenomenon of group selection because evolution of the peculiar characteristics of various forms of communication, through language, through law, through morals and the market, is based on the fact that not only a single individual, but all the members of a group acquire certain characteristics.

Few aspects of Hayek's thought have inspired more objections than his cultural evolutionism. Not only does it raise formidable logical, philosophical, and anthropological problems, its celebration of traditional practices seems quite restrictive. Marx has spoken of history as a dead hand impeding progress. Hayek saw in it an irreplaceable helping hand from the past. His evolutionism emphasizes that our cultural institutions tell us what has worked for earlier generations, without our having to know what the actual circumstances may have been. Our traditional moral code, for example, is derived from the experience and practices of the generations that precede us. It requires us to accept on faith such values as honesty, keeping our word, and respecting other persons and their property. The reward for observing this code that no one invented, says Hayek, is a benefit no one intended: human freedom.

> Freedom has been made possible by the restraint of freedom. Primitive man, in his small band, was by no means free. He was bound to follow the predominant emotions of his group, he couldn't move away from his group, freedom just did not exist under natural conditions. Freedom is an artifact. Again, the word artifact is the one we currently use but it is not a result of design, not of deliberate creation, but of cultural evolution.

Hayek's "evolutionism" appeared to set him farther apart than ever from prevailing intellectual trends. Where he was talking about concealed wisdom in our cultural institutions, others were focusing on the contradictions and outright harm embedded in traditional practices. And his views seemed irrelevant to the postwar generation. Their subculture expressed an impatience with the existent order in its music, morals, and lifestyles. Hayek was aware of his isolation, and, as ever, put his faith in the long run:

> Two things happened in the last hundred years. On the one hand, a steadily-increasing part of the population did no longer learn in daily life the rules of the market on which our civilization is based, because they grew up in organizations, rather than participating in the market.

They no longer were taught these rules. At the same time, the intellectuals began to tell them these rules are nonsense anyhow, they are irrational, don't believe in that nonsense. And the combination of these two effects — on the one hand, people were no longer learning the rules, and on the other hand, a sort of Cartesian rationalism which told them "don't accept anything you do not understand" — collaborated, and this produced the present situation, where there is already a lack of supporting moral belief which is required to maintain our civilization.

As he entered his seventies, Hayek's thought was finally finding an audience. To many, he was beginning to appear as a prophet of the difficulties now facing governments in both Europe and North America. The economic policies that had performed so brilliantly just a few years earlier no longer seemed effective against rising inflation and unemployment. The failure of these policies led some groups to demand more radical measures. But a growing conservative movement was determined to draw the line. The intellectuals of the New Right seized on the political potential of Hayek's ideas. The Nobel Prize in 1974 was one measure of his rehabilitation. His popularity with Margaret Thatcher's Conservatives in Britain was another. Now, when he visited London, he was an honoured guest at 10 Downing Street. The 1980s brought a more ironic vindication. Eastern Europe discovered Hayek. Circulating on videotape and manuscript, his ideas met with fervent interest among people who had given up on the social and economic experiments of Marxism. Long before the fall of the Berlin Wall, Hayek had become an important intellectual influence in circles opposed to the communist regimes.

Hayek savoured the irony that one of the unintended consequences of forty years of communist rule in the East was the creation of a social and intellectual climate receptive to his ideas. He was, after all, one of the first to analyse in detail the reasons central planning would not and could not work. At the outset, few were convinced by his argument. After 1945 the regimes of Eastern

Europe were embarked on an experiment whose outcome seemed far from clear in its early days. By 1989, however, the experiment had demonstrated to the satisfaction of almost everyone in Eastern Europe that a relatively unplanned, relatively uncentralized economy works better. Hayek's appeal went deeper than just being right about the failure of communism, however.

People in Eastern Europe, in the years before the fall of the Wall, were searching for something more than a mere negative attack on the socialist system by which they were surrounded. They wanted a philosophy, or at least a political theory, that would give the concepts whereby some alternative could be founded. In Hayek, especially in the later writings, Eastern Europeans found much of value, partly because they had lost so much in the way of law and tradition and the role of institutions generally. Hayek offered an attempt to integrate the free market into a comprehensive vision of human society. Thus Hayek became extremely popular among certain sections of the opposition to communism, many of whose members are now in power.

This attraction to Hayek by many Eastern Europeans must be accounted as strange. There can be little doubt that many Eastern Europeans seek a society based on many of the institutions Hayek has always regarded as central. But can Hayek the evolutionist have anything to say to such people? How can evolution help those struggling to recover from forty years of a regime dedicated to stamping out many of the grown institutions Hayek so values, things like law and the market? After all, little serious law remains after forty years of communism. On a deeper level, many of the states of mind, many of the moral values on which modern civilization depends, have been jeopardized. The notion of personal responsibility for one's actions, for example, or respect for property, or rewarding hard work through inequalities in income, are all ideas that have been under sustained attack.

Many Eastern bloc political leaders remain optimistic, even in the face of these difficulties. They know they must try to design the legal and other frameworks from which institutions like the market and real law will emerge, and that this must appear a paradox from a Hayekian point of view. The paradox, however, is more apparent than real. The real challenge is to help people in these countries make the link between a dimly recollected past and the world of today. As politician after politician I spoke to in Eastern Europe told me, it is not a question of inventing a new society from scratch, no more than it is a question of introducing contract and property to societies that have never known them. The question is how to sweep away the damage to such institutions and practices caused by a forty-year aberration. Once some basic legal institutions are in place that provide some stability and certainty for individual decision-making, then the initiative and ingenuity of Eastern Europeans themselves will fill in the rest. The stops and starts of reform over the coming years will reflect the difficulty of feeling one's way forward. There are, however, no shortcuts through this learning process, in which forty years of lost adjustment to new knowledge must be made up. In the meantime, the great danger is that the patience of long-suffering peoples will be exhausted and an authoritarian alternative to the market order will exercise a fatal attraction.

In the West, the high tide of the New Right's influence seems now to have passed. Deregulation, privatization, and other market reforms have become political commonplaces, and the fervour of reform seems largely to have spent itself. Is there a future for Hayekian ideas in the 1990s? Many seem convinced that our problems are of an order such that Hayek's solutions seem simplistic or positively pernicious.

Take the environment. The problems of pollution and environmental degradation seem daily to assume such proportions that Hayek's faith in individual responsibility and initiative within a system of market-transmitted information may seem a weak response indeed. Part of the problem of the environment is precisely that in the past markets have treated the environment as without economicvalue, and so information about it was not embodied in prices. Also, the scale of the problem seems to suggest that we cannot afford the further damage that a long-run experimental approach to dealing with the environment requires. If, for example, global warming is occurring on the popular model, then it is occurring as a result of billions and billions of individual acts. Each of those acts has little side effect, but when taken together, they result in an impact on the environment that is seriously harmful.

This underestimates the power of the Hayekian approach. Hayek would argue that our environmental problems arise from our failure to bring the environment within the pale of spontaneously grown institutions, and to treat it as something with economic value. The key here is to extend the grown order of property rights to the environment: if the economy has not taken account of the costs of environmental degradation in the past, it is because nobody had economic interests to protect when the air and water were polluted.

A similar approach, now being experimented with in the United States, is to create a market in pollution itself. To make the logic of the market work for the environment the government can create what might be called "pollution permits," tradeable bits of paper authorizing the emission of a given quantity and type of pollutant. As long as the supply of such permits is limited, and anyone polluting without one can be sued or fined, the value of the permits will steadily increase. This will put ever greater economic pressure on polluters to reduce pollution, because pollution itself will now have a measurable, direct, and increasing economic cost to them. By the same token, those opposed to pollution will have the opportunity to take direct and concrete action by banding together to buy permits and taking them out of circulation. Each permit so retired raises the cost of polluting and, therefore, the incentive to find non-polluting ways to carry out one's business.

When we step back from particular issues in Hayek's now influential thought and attempt to assess his life and work, one cannot help but savour an irony. Hayek's great quest was to make people realize the limits of the human mind relative to the complexity of human society. He tried, with mixed success, to call our attention to the intellectual arrogance and presumption of the great ideologies that have so dominated our century: Nazism, Stalinism, radical feminism, communism, Marxism, and nationalism, to name but a few. He tirelessly reminded us that all such grandiose plans to reconstruct society nearer to our heart's desire must flounder on our limited knowledge, on the fact that all our actions have consequences we cannot foresee and, therefore, cannot plan for and control as we might wish.

But in Hayek's efforts to make this message plain, he may have fallen victim to the weakness he so eloquently denounced in others. He appears to have taken a philosophy that celebrates the unplanned, the unconscious, the incremental, the practical, and made it into a grand abstract and theoretical construct. All that is worthwhile can be reduced to the twin concepts of spontaneous order and cultural evolutionism.

Still, his critics often make a parody of his thought, suggesting that he sees no role for human reason, for conscious human effort directed at improving our condition. His position, however, has never been that. Rather, he always strove to draw out the fact that civilization is a never ending dialogue between the hopes and desires of the present and the accumulated wisdom of the past.

The much more telling criticism of Hayek is that his optimism about the benevolence of spontaneously grown institutions may well be unjustified, and that our institutions are not a helping hand from the past. After all, maybe Keynes was right in at least one thing, that the image of an invisible hand ordering markets for the social good was implausible. Perhaps it is as much an invisible boot as an invisible hand, and there is limited justification even for the qualified optimism espoused by Hayek.

That subtracts nothing, however, from Hayek's great practical accomplishments. He has shown us, in a convincing modern idiom, that markets can often do what governments and central planning cannot: they can, when they operate against the backdrop of a proper set of legal institutions, yield prosperity without sacrificing freedom. The result is that Hayek has made many people less pessimistic in their judgements of markets than they were even a few short years ago, and he's made us more pessimistic about what governments can achieve.

The fact remains, however, that there are many problems, such as nuclear proliferation, international terrorism, and perhaps global environmental degradation that neither governments *nor* markets can really influence satisfactorily. Markets may be better than we thought, and governments rather worse. The reality is that the case for caution and skepticism about *all* human institutions is much stronger than is the case for Hayek's optimism based on an unprovable faith. Perhaps the most judicious appreciation of Hayek's work was George Orwell's, that it is in the negative part of Hayek's argument that we find the greater truth.

LIST OF CONTRIBUTORS

Norman Barry, University of Buckingham
Alec Cairncross, Oxford University
Meghnad Desai, London School of Economics
Ernest Gellner, Cambridge University
John Gray, Oxford University
Ralph Harris, Institute for Economic Affairs
Thomas Jezek, Government Minister, Prague
Kari Levitt, McGill University
Madsen Pirie, Adam Smith Institute, London
John Redwood, Government Minister, London

Roger Scruton, University of London
Georg Tintner, Halifax
Andrej Zawislak, Deputy Speaker, Sejm (Parliament), Warsaw

Note: All of the displayed quotations in this piece are from my own transcriptions of interviews, speeches, or discussions by or with F. A. Hayek.